Book Y2

CAMBRIDGE
UNIVERSITY PRESS

Published by the Press Syndicate of the University of Cambridge
The Pitt Building, Trumpington Street, Cambridge CB2 1RP
40 West 20th Street, New York, NY 10011–4211, USA
10 Stamford Road, Oakleigh, Victoria 3166, Australia

First published 1985

Seventh printing 1992

Illustrations by David Parkins
Diagrams and phototypesetting by Parkway Group, London
and Abingdon, and Gecko Limited, Bicester, Oxon.

Printed in Great Britain at the University Press, Cambridge

British Library cataloguing in publication data

SMP 11–16 yellow series.
  Bk Y2
  1. Mathematics – 1961 –
  I. School Mathematics Project
  510   QA39.2
  ISBN 0 521 31674X

Acknowledgements
The authors and the publisher would like to thank the following
for permission to use copyright material: M. C. Escher,
'Ascending and descending' (front cover; Gemeentemuseum,
The Hague) and 'Belvedere' (Rijksmuseum, Amsterdam), © M.
C. Escher Heirs c/o Cordon Art – Baarn – Holland; 'Roger
Haward's undecidable monument', *Wormrunner's digest*,
December 1968; Penrose triangle, Professor R. L. Gregory,
Brain and Perception Laboratory, University of Bristol; graphs
of tides, D. H. Macmillan, *Tides* CR Books Ltd 1966

Contents

1 Relationships

A Graphs

There are many circumstances in everyday life where one quantity
is related to another.

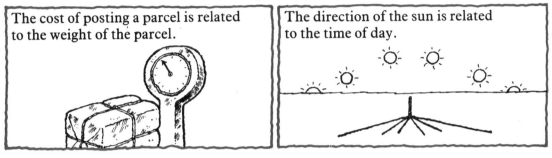

The cost of posting a parcel is related
to the weight of the parcel.

The direction of the sun is related
to the time of day.

Often one quantity is related to several other quantities.

The cost of a phone call is related to
the distance, the length of the call,
the day of the week and the time of day.

The amount of petrol a car uses is related
to the distance travelled, the speed, the size
of the engine, and many other things.

In this chapter we shall be studying examples where one quantity is
related to **one** other quantity.

The relationship between two quantities can be shown in a graph.

This graph shows how the
length of daylight in London
is related to the time of year.

(The time of year is measured
in weeks from 1st January
onwards.)

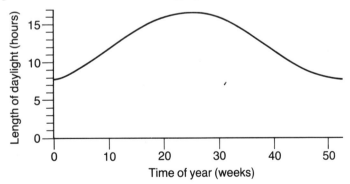

A1 Describe briefly in words how the number of hours of daylight
changes as you go through the year.

1

Variables

A quantity whose value can change is called a **variable**.
A graph shows how one variable is related to another variable.

The graph on the previous page shows how the
variable 'length of daylight' is related to
the variable 'time of year'.

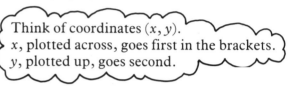

'Time of year' was plotted **across**.
'Length of daylight' was plotted **up**.

So we call the graph

the graph of (time of year, length of daylight).

> Think of coordinates (x, y).
> x, plotted across, goes first in the brackets.
> y, plotted up, goes second.

We could use letters to stand for the variables.

Suppose we use t for 'time of year', and d for
'length of daylight'.

The graph would then be called the graph of
(t, d).

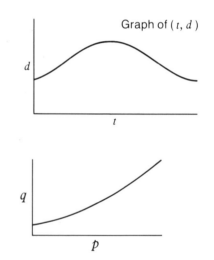

A2 p and q are two variables, and
this graph shows how q is related
to p.
As p increases, so q increases.

Draw sketch graphs showing two variables p and q related
in these ways (sketch a graph of (p, q) in each case).
(a) As p increases, so q decreases.
(b) As p increases, so q decreases at first, then increases.
(c) As p increases, so q stays constant (neither increasing
    nor decreasing).
(d) As p increases, so q increases at first, then decreases.

A3 A train travels between two stations. It starts from rest (speed zero).
Its speed increases until it reaches a maximum. The train travels
at this maximum speed for a while and then it slows down to a stop.
The time taken at the beginning to reach the maximum speed is greater
than the time taken to slow down to a stop. Sketch a graph of (time, speed).

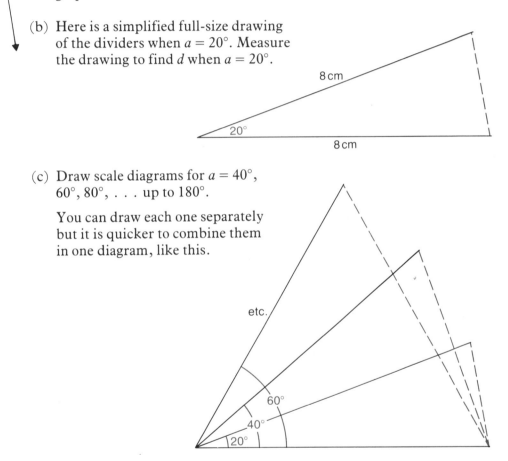

A4 The diagram on the left shows a pair of 'dividers'.

(It is like a pair of compasses except that it has two points instead of one point and a pencil. Dividers are used for marking off lengths on drawings.)

The distance, *d* cm, between the two points is related to the angle *a*.

(a) Think of what happens to the distance *d* as the angle *a* is increased from 0° to 180°. What do you think the graph of (*a*, *d*) will look like? Draw a sketch to show roughly what shape you expect the graph to be.

(b) Here is a simplified full-size drawing of the dividers when *a* = 20°. Measure the drawing to find *d* when *a* = 20°.

(c) Draw scale diagrams for *a* = 40°, 60°, 80°, . . . up to 180°.

You can draw each one separately but it is quicker to combine them in one diagram, like this.

Make a table showing values of *a* and *d*.

a	0°	20°	40°	80°	100°	. . . up to 180°
d						

(d) Draw a graph of (*a*, *d*). Compare it with your sketch.

(e) What will happen to *d* as *a* is increased still more, from 180° to 360°? Draw a sketch graph to show what happens.

3

B Discontinuous graphs

This is the dial of a parcel weighing machine. It shows the cost (in 1985) of sending parcels by post.

For parcels weighing up to 1 kg, the postage is £1·33. Then the postage jumps to £1·72 for parcels weighing from 1 kg to 2 kg.

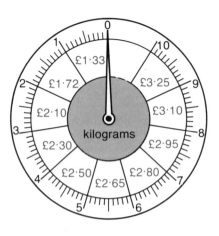

The graph of (weight, postage) looks like this.

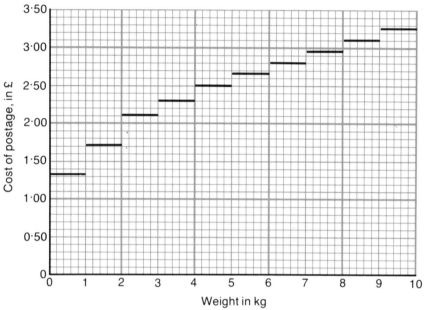

A graph like this with 'jumps' in it is called a **discontinuous** graph.

B1 This table shows the 2nd class letter postage rates in 1985.

Weight in grams	Cost in pence	Weight in grams	Cost in pence
0– 60	13	300–350	46
60–100	18	350–400	52
100–150	22	400–450	59
150–200	28	450–500	66
200–250	34	500–750	98
250–300	40		

Draw a graph of (weight, cost of postage).

B2 A taxi service charges 90p for distances up to 2 km, then an extra 50p for every extra kilometre. (An extra part of a kilometre counts as 1 km, so a journey of 3·2 km counts as 4 km.)
Draw a graph of (distance, cost of journey) for distances up to 6 km.

B3 The graph below shows the number of people in the queue at a supermarket checkout (including the person being served). Every time someone joins the queue, the graph jumps up by 1. Every time someone leaves, the graph jumps down by 1. (We assume that no two people join and leave at exactly the same instant.)

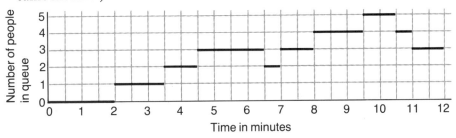

(a) At what times did people join the queue?

(b) Nobody left the queue before being served. How long did it take to serve the first person who came along?

B4 Here is some information about another queue.
Draw a graph for this queue (like the one in question B3).

To start with there is nobody in the queue.
People join the queue at 1·5, 2·5, 4, 5·5, 6·5, 7 and 11 minutes.
People leave the queue at 3, 5, 8, 8·5, 9·5, 10·5 and 12 minutes.

Here is another kind of discontinuous graph.

This graph shows how the size of the angles in a regular polygon is related to the number of sides. (For example, a 5-sided regular polygon has angles of 108°.)

The number of sides can only be a whole number (from 3 upwards), so the graph consists of a set of isolated points.

B5 Draw a polygon with 5 sides.
Choose one corner and draw all the diagonals from that corner. You will find that you have split the polygon into 3 triangles.

Draw polygons with different numbers of sides. In each case, choose a corner and draw all the diagonals from it.

Draw a graph of (number of sides, number of triangles).

5

C Linear and non-linear relationships

From now on in this chapter, all graphs will be continuous.

A **linear** relationship is one whose graph is a **single straight line**.
These graphs show linear relationships between q and p.

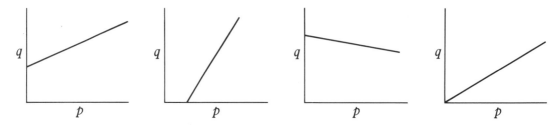

The graphs below show **non-linear** relationships.

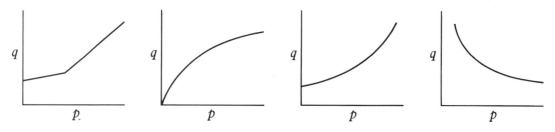

When there is a **linear** relationship between q and p . . .

if p goes up by equal amounts,
so q goes up by equal amounts,   **or**   if p goes up by equal amounts,
so q goes down by equal amounts.

This does not happen in a **non-linear** relationship.
Here, as p changes by equal amounts, q does not.

C1 This table shows the length of a spring when different weights hang from it.

Weight in grams	40	60	80	100	120	140	160
Length in cm	6·6	8·4	10·2	12·0	13·8	15·6	17·4

(a) In the table the weight goes up by equal amounts each time. Is this true of the length as well? Is the relationship between length and weight linear?

(b) Draw a graph of (weight, length).

(c) Use the graph to find
  (i) the length when the weight is 105 g
  (ii) the weight when the length is 10·6 cm.

C2 (a) How can you tell from this table that the relationship between q and p is non-linear?

p	15	20	25	30	35	40	45
q	7	13	18	22	25	27	28

(b) Draw a graph of (p, q).

C3 (a) How can you tell that this table shows a linear relationship between s and r?

r	8	10	12	14	16	18	20
s	31	27	23	19	15	11	7

(b) Draw a graph of (r, s).

C4 For every 500 feet you go up a mountain, the temperature drops by 1 °C.

(a) Is the relationship between temperature and height linear?

(b) Make a rough sketch to show the shape of the graph of (height, temperature).

In this table **neither** variable goes up in equal steps.

p	12	20	26	28	36	42
q	30	42	51	54	66	75

So you cannot tell from the table above whether the relationship is linear or non-linear. But you can find out by drawing a graph.

C5 (a) Draw a graph of (p, q) from the table above. Is the relationship between p and q linear or non-linear?

(b) Use the graph to complete the table below, in which p does go up in equal steps. You should find that q goes up in equal steps as well.

p	10	20	30	40
q				

D Proportionality

<table>
<tr>
<td>Think of a glass cylinder which starts empty.</td>
<td>Water is poured in.
As the height of the water level goes up by equal amounts, so the volume of the water goes up by equal amounts.</td>
</tr>
</table>

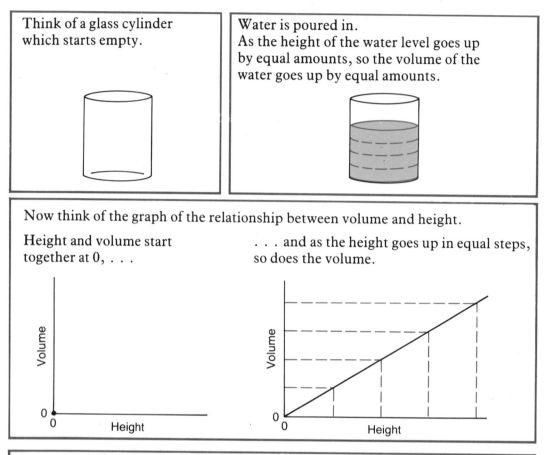

Now think of the graph of the relationship between volume and height.

Height and volume start together at 0, . . .

. . . and as the height goes up in equal steps, so does the volume.

The graph is a straight line through $(0, 0)$.
We say the volume **is proportional to** the height. This is a special kind of linear relationship where **the graph is a straight line through $(0, 0)$.**

Here are two more examples of porportionality.

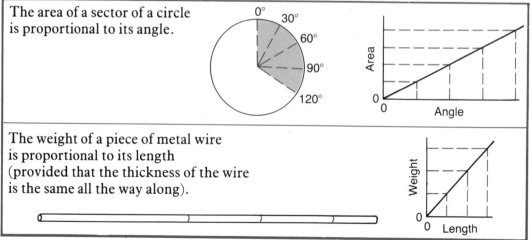

The area of a sector of a circle is proportional to its angle.

The weight of a piece of metal wire is proportional to its length (provided that the thickness of the wire is the same all the way along).

Here are two examples of **non-proportionality**.

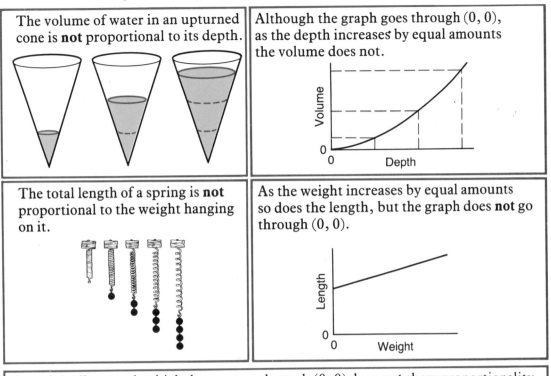

The volume of water in an upturned cone is **not** proportional to its depth.

Although the graph goes through $(0, 0)$, as the depth increases by equal amounts the volume does not.

The total length of a spring is **not** proportional to the weight hanging on it.

As the weight increases by equal amounts so does the length, but the graph does **not** go through $(0, 0)$.

A straight-line graph which does **not** go through $(0, 0)$ does **not** show proportionality.

D1 In which of these graphs is q proportional to p?

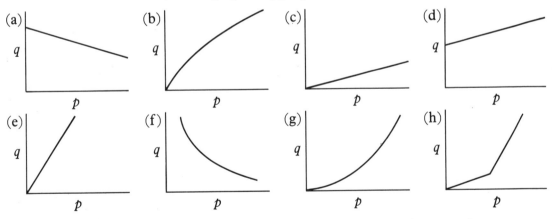

(a) (b) (c) (d)

(e) (f) (g) (h)

D2 (a) Copy and complete this table showing the perimeters of squares.

Side of square, in cm	0	3	4	7	10
Perimeter of square, in cm					

(b) Draw the graph of (side, perimeter).
(c) Is the perimeter of a square proportional to its side?

D3 Repeat question D2 for the side and area of a square.

When you buy a quantity of something, sometimes the cost is proportional to the quantity, and sometimes not.

Suppose you buy dress material which costs £3 a metre.

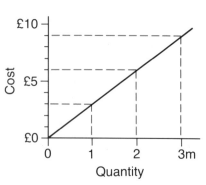

Every metre you buy costs the same, and the graph of (quantity, cost) is **a straight line through (0, 0)**.

(It goes through (0, 0) because if you buy 0 metres you pay £0.)

In this case **the cost is proportional to the quantity.**

Now look at these prices of bags of crisps in a supermarket.

Weight	25 g	50 g	75 g
Cost	15p	25p	30p

If the cost were proportional to the quantity, we would expect a 50 g bag to cost the same as two 25 g bags, which would be 30p. But in fact the extra 25 g costs only 10p. And if we buy a 75 g bag, we get the next 25 g for only 5p.

The graph of (quantity, cost) looks like this.

It goes through (0, 0) because 0 g costs 0p. But it is **not** a straight line.

The cost here is **not** proportional to the quantity.

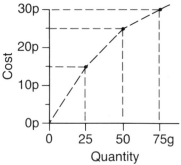

D4 When a motorist buys petrol from a petrol pump, is the cost proportional to the quantity?

D5 These are the prices a garden centre charges for grass seed.

Quantity of seed	Cost
3 lb	£1·35
5 lb	£2·25
10 lb	£4·50
12 lb	£4·80
25 lb	£9·00
60 lb	£19·90

Is the cost of grass seed proportional to the quantity bought?

D6 This diagram shows distances and single fares (in 1985) from London to some stations on the main line to the south-west.

London Paddington		
Slough	$18\frac{1}{2}$ miles	£2·30
Reading	36 miles	£4·30
Newbury	53 miles	£5·70
Westbury	$95\frac{1}{2}$ miles	£12·40

(a) Draw axes labelled 'distance in miles' across and 'single fare in £' up. Plot the points for the four stations.
(b) Is the fare proportional to the distance?
(c) Which station has the cheapest fare in relation to its distance?
(d) Which has the most expensive fare in relation to its distance?

D7 A searchlight shines a beam of light on to a vertical wall.
The searchlight is 50 m from the wall.

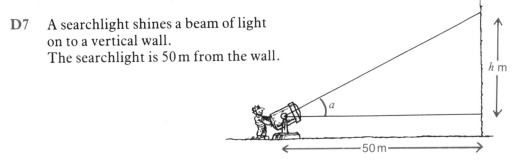

a stands for the angle which the beam makes with the horizontal.
h is the height in metres of the point where the beam hits the wall, measured from the level of the searchlight.

(a) Draw scale diagrams to find h when a is 15°, 30°, 45°, 60°.

Make a table.

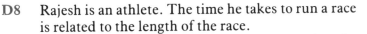

a	0°	15°	30°	45°	60°
h					

(b) Draw a graph of (a, h).
(c) Is h proportional to a?

D8 Rajesh is an athlete. The time he takes to run a race is related to the length of the race.

(a) Which of these graphs is most likely to show how the time taken is related to the length of the race?

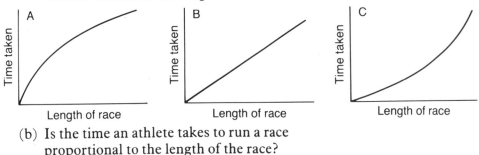

(b) Is the time an athlete takes to run a race proportional to the length of the race?

2 Accuracy

A Interval approximations: addition and subtraction

The numbers given for the populations of countries can never be exactly correct.
People are dying, being born, emigrating and so on, all the time.
Approximate numbers and estimates are often given in the form
'between . . . and . . .'. For example, the population of France is between
50 million and 60 million.

We say the population of France lies in the **interval** 50 million to 60 million.
The length, or size, of this interval is 60 million − 50 million = 10 million.

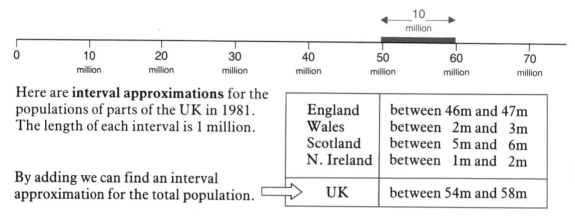

Here are **interval approximations** for the
populations of parts of the UK in 1981.
The length of each interval is 1 million.

England	between 46m and 47m
Wales	between 2m and 3m
Scotland	between 5m and 6m
N. Ireland	between 1m and 2m

By adding we can find an interval
approximation for the total population.

| UK | between 54m and 58m |

Notice how rough this approximation for the total is. The length of the interval
is 4 million. For each separate part of the UK the length is only 1 million.

A1 Here are interval approximations for the numbers of people in
different age groups in the UK in 1981.

Age group	Number of people
0– 4	between 3·4m and 3·5m
5–14	8·1m 8·2m
15–44	23·6m 23·7m
45–59	9·4m 9·5m
60–64	2·9m 3·0m
65 and over	8·3m 8·4m

(a) What is the length of the interval for the number in each group?
(b) Calculate an interval approximation for the total population.
(c) What is the length of the interval you have given for the total?

A2 Each side of a square is between 4·7 and 4·8 metres long.
Give an interval approximation for the perimeter of the square.

In 1931, the population of the UK was between 46 million and 47 million.
In 1981, it was between 55 million and 56 million.

This diagram illustrates the two intervals.

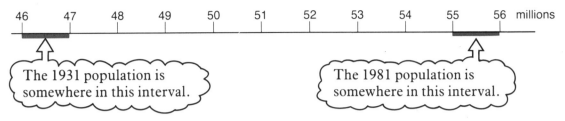

The population increased from somewhere between 46m and 47m
to somewhere between 55m and 56m.

The increase would be smallest if the population had been 47m in 1931
and 55m in 1981. This is an increase of 8m.

The increase would be greatest if the population had been 46m in 1931
and 56m in 1981. This is an increase of 10m.

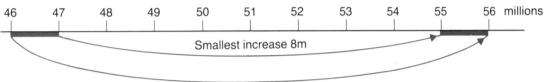

So the population increase was **between 8 million and 10 million**.

A3 In 1901, the population of a town was between 69 000 and 70 000.
In 1951, it was between 123 000 and 124 000.
Give an interval approximation for the increase in population.

A4 The population of the USA is between 231m and 232m.
The population of the USSR is between 264m and 265m.
Give an interval approximation for the difference between the
two populations.

A5 A machine makes red plastic strips whose lengths are in the interval
23·5 cm to 24·5 cm. Another machine makes black strips whose lengths
are in the interval 17·5 cm to 18·5 cm.

(a) If we put one of the red strips and one of the black strips end to end,
what are the minimum and maximum possible values of the
total length?

(b) If we put a red strip and a black strip side by side, what are the
minimum and maximum possible values of the difference in length?

13

Tolerances

Suppose a machine is meant to make bolts which are 6·3 cm long.
It is not practically possible to have a machine which will make every bolt
exactly 6·3 cm long. But it may be good enough if the length is in the
interval 6·25 cm to 6·35 cm.

The difference between the upper and lower limits of the length is called
the **tolerance**. In this case it is 6·35 cm − 6·25 cm = 0·1 cm.

The interval from 6·25 to 6·35 can be described in another way.

The centre of the interval is 6·3.
The lower end is 6·25, which is 6·3 − 0·05.
The upper end is 6·35, which is 6·3 + 0·05.

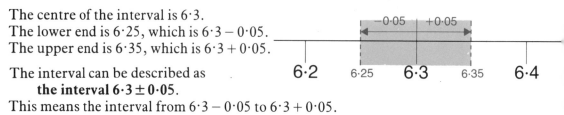

The interval can be described as
the interval 6·3 ± 0·05.
This means the interval from 6·3 − 0·05 to 6·3 + 0·05.

This method of describing intervals is often used in technical work.

A6 A more accurate machine makes bolts with lengths in the interval
6·3 ± 0·02 cm. Write this interval in the form 'between . . . and . . .'

A7 Write the interval between 5·75 and 5·85 in the form $a \pm b$.

A8 Write each of these intervals in the form 'between . . . and . . .'
(a) 8·8 ± 0·05   (b) 7·64 ± 0·005   (c) 7·6 ± 0·05
(d) 3·0 ± 0·05   (e) 10·8 ± 0·01   (f) 2·80 ± 0·005

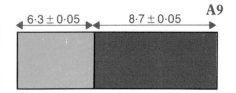

A9 Two metal blocks are placed together.
The length of the first is in the interval 6·3 ± 0·05 cm.
The length of the second is in the interval 8·7 ± 0·05 cm.

Calculate an interval approximation for the
total length, in the form 'between . . . and . . .'

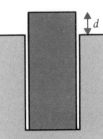

A10 During a manufacturing process, one machine drills a cavity in a
metal block and another machine makes a plastic plug which drops
into the cavity.

The depth of the cavity can be anywhere in the interval 29 ± 0·5 mm.
The length of the plug can be anywhere in the interval 35 ± 0·5 mm.

If d is the distance by which the plug protrudes from the cavity,
find the minimum and maximum possible values of d.

B Interval approximations: multiplication and division

A rectangular hall is between 25 metres and
26 metres long, and between 17 m and 18 m wide.
The diagram shows its minimum and maximum
dimensions.

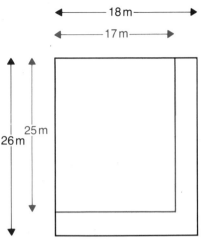

Its area must be between 25×17 sq m and
26×18 sq m, that is, between **425** and **468** sq m.

Notice how rough this approximation is.
The size of the interval is $468 - 425 = 43$ sq m.

When you multiply two rough approximations
together, you get a **very** rough approximation.

B1 The length of a rectangle is between 3·6 m and 3·7 m.
The width is between 1·7 m and 1·8 m.
Calculate an interval approximation for the area of the rectangle.

B2 The volume of a block of plastic is between 340 and 350 cubic cm.
1 cubic cm of the plastic weighs between 2·8 and 2·9 grams.
Calculate an interval approximation for the weight of the block.

B3 A machine is supposed to make plastic blocks 3 cm by 3 cm by 3 cm.
The machine is not accurate, and the length, width and height
of the blocks it makes can be anywhere between 2·9 cm and 3·1 cm.

Calculate an interval approximation for the volume of the blocks.

B4 On a tin of paint it says '1 litre will cover between 12 and 15
square metres, depending on the absorbency of the surface'.
I have to paint a wall whose area is 240 square metres, but I have
no idea how absorbent it is. What are the minimum and maximum
amounts of paint I might need?

B5 An amount of money, which could be anything from £300 to £400,
is to be shared equally by a group of people, who could number anything
from 10 to 20 people.

(a) What is the minimum possible amount one person could receive?

(b) How did you calculate the minimum amount per person?
(What did you divide by what?)

(c) What is the maximum possible amount per person?

(d) How did you calculate the maximum amount per person?

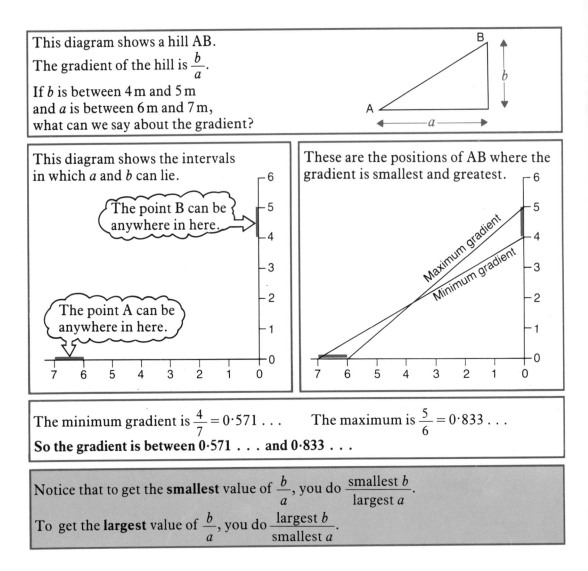

This diagram shows a hill AB.

The gradient of the hill is $\dfrac{b}{a}$.

If b is between 4 m and 5 m
and a is between 6 m and 7 m,
what can we say about the gradient?

This diagram shows the intervals in which a and b can lie.

The point B can be anywhere in here.

The point A can be anywhere in here.

These are the positions of AB where the gradient is smallest and greatest.

Maximum gradient

Minimum gradient

The minimum gradient is $\dfrac{4}{7} = 0\cdot571\ldots$ The maximum is $\dfrac{5}{6} = 0\cdot833\ldots$

So the gradient is between $0\cdot571\ldots$ and $0\cdot833\ldots$

Notice that to get the **smallest** value of $\dfrac{b}{a}$, you do $\dfrac{\text{smallest } b}{\text{largest } a}$.

To get the **largest** value of $\dfrac{b}{a}$, you do $\dfrac{\text{largest } b}{\text{smallest } a}$.

B6   If a is between 9 and 10, and b is between 5 and 6,

calculate   (a) the smallest value of $\dfrac{b}{a}$ (b) the largest value of $\dfrac{b}{a}$

(c) the smallest value of $\dfrac{a}{b}$ (d) the largest value of $\dfrac{a}{b}$

B7   If r is between $1\cdot5$ and $1\cdot6$, and s is between $2\cdot4$ and $2\cdot5$,

calculate   (a) the largest value of $\dfrac{r}{s}$ (b) the smallest value of $\dfrac{s}{r}$

(c) the smallest value of $\dfrac{r}{s}$ (d) the largest value of $\dfrac{s}{r}$

c Rounding

This is a close-up of some pieces of wire being measured in centimetres.

Their lengths are wanted to the **nearest tenth of a centimetre**.

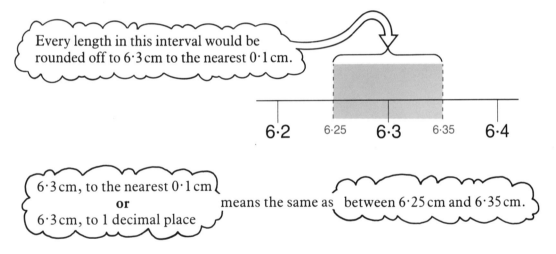

When the lengths are rounded to the nearest tenths mark,
A is 6·2 cm;   B, C, D and E are all 6·3 cm;   F is 6·4 cm.

The boundary between rounding down and rounding up is halfway between each pair of tenths marks.

Every length in this interval would be rounded off to 6·3 cm to the nearest 0·1 cm.

6·2   6·25   6·3   6·35   6·4

6·3 cm, to the nearest 0·1 cm
or
6·3 cm, to 1 decimal place

means the same as   between 6·25 cm and 6·35 cm.

(Strictly speaking, if we follow the rule that numbers ending in a 5 are to be rounded up, then we should not include 6·35 itself in the interval, because 6·35 itself would be rounded up to 6·4. However, this point is of no practical importance in the work which follows, and will be ignored.)

When you **round off** a number, you are really giving an **interval approximation**.

For example, suppose a town's population is given as 7400, to the nearest hundred. Think of the number line, with numbers marked in hundreds.

Halfway between 7300 and 7400 is **7350**.

Halfway between 7400 and 7500 is **7450**.

So the interval is **between 7350 and 7450**.

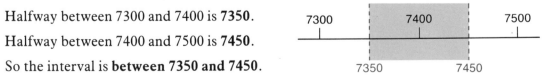

7300   7400   7500

7350   7450

17

Worked examples

(1) Write as an interval approximation: 7·264 to 3 d.p.

Think of the number line, with numbers marked to 3 d.p.
The numbers either side of 7·264 are 7·263 and 7·265.

Halfway between 7·263 and 7·264 is **7·2635**.
Halfway between 7·264 and 7·265 is **7·2645**.
So the interval is **between 7·2635 and 7·2645**.

(2) Write as an interval approximation: 6·20 to 3 significant figures.

Think of the number line, with numbers marked to 3 s.f.
The numbers either side of 6·20 are 6·19 and 6·21.

Halfway between 6·19 and 6·20 is **6·195**.
Halfway between 6·20 and 6·21 is **6·205**.
So the interval is **between 6·195 and 6·205**.

C1 A book gives the density of mercury as 13·6 grams per cubic centimetre, to 1 decimal place. Write this as an interval approximation, in the form between 'between . . . and . . .'

C2 Write each of these as an interval approximation.
    (a) 4·8 to 1 d.p.   (b) 197 000 to the nearest thousand
    (c) 0·046 to 3 d.p.   (d) 3·80 to 2 d.p.   (e) 5·95 to 2 d.p.
    (f) 4·0 to 1 d.p.   (g) 7·310 to 3 d.p.   (h) 3·00 to 2 d.p.

Diameter in mm	Resistance in ohms per m
0·02	54·9
0·1	2·20
0·2	0·549
0·5	0·0879

C3 The table on the left gives the electrical resistance (in ohms per metre) of copper wire of various thicknesses. The resistances are each given to 3 significant figures.

Write down an interval approximation for each of the four resistances.

C4 The population of city A is 284 000, to the nearest thousand.
The population of city B is 431 000, to the nearest thousand.

    (a) Write down interval approximations for the population of A and for the population of B .
    (b) Write down an interval approximation for the total population of the two cities.
    (c) Is it true to say that the total population, to the nearest thousand, is 284 000 + 431 000 = 715 000, to the nearest thousand?
    (d) Is it true to say that the total difference in population, to the nearest thousand, is 431 000 − 284 000 = 147 000? Explain.

D The effect of rounding on calculations

If the numbers in a calculation are only approximations, then the
result can only be an approximation too.
Here is an example to illustrate this.

A car travelled along a section of test track.
The distance travelled was 300 m, to the nearest metre.
The time taken was 8·3 seconds, to the nearest 0·1 second.

The speed of the car is wanted, as accurately as
the measurements allow.

First we can write down interval approximations for the distance and time.

The distance was between 299·5 m and 300·5 m.
The time was between 8·25 seconds and 8·35 seconds.

The speed would be lowest if the car
had gone the shortest possible distance
in the longest possible time.

So the lowest value of the speed is
$\frac{299·5}{8·35}$ m/s = **35·868 . . . m/s.**

The speed would be highest if the car
had gone the longest possible distance
in the shortest possible time.

So the highest value of the speed is
$\frac{300·5}{8·25}$ m/s = **36·424 . . . m/s.**

So the speed is between 35·868 . . . m/s and 36·424 . . . m/s.
A reasonable 'rounded off' value would be **36 m/s to the nearest 1 m/s.**

Now see what happens if you treat the original measurements as exact.

The speed would be $\frac{300}{8·3}$ m/s = 36·144 . . . m/s.

You might be tempted to round this off to, say, 2 decimal places.
But that would not be right at all. As we have seen above, the speed
could be anywhere between 35·868 . . . m/s and 36·424 . . . m/s.

D1 A high speed train on a test run covered a distance of
750 metres (measured correct to the nearest metre)
in a time of 12·4 seconds (measured correct to the
nearest 0·1 second).

(a) Calculate the lowest and highest possible values of
the speed of the train.
(b) Give a reasonable rounded off value for the speed.

D2 The sides of a rectangular field are measured to the
nearest metre. They are 343 m and 213 m.
(a) Write down each measurement as an interval approximation.
(b) Calculate the smallest and largest possible values of the
area of the field, in sq m. (Notice how far apart they are.)
(c) Give a reasonable rounded off value for the area.

A 'rule of thumb'

It would be tedious to calculate smallest and largest possible values in every calculation based on approximate numbers.
The following 'rule of thumb' is not always correct, but it usually gives reasonable results.

> When you multiply or divide, give the result to as many significant figures as there are in the **least** accurate of the numbers used.

For example, suppose a is $2\cdot36$ to 3 s.f. and b is $0\cdot041$ to 2 s.f.
and you want a reasonable value for ab.
First calculate ab as if the numbers were exact: $2\cdot36 \times 0\cdot041 = 0\cdot09676$.
The least accurate of the numbers is b, which is given to 2 s.f.
So round off your value of ab to 2 s.f. So $ab = \mathbf{0\cdot097}$ **to 2 s.f.**

D3 If $p = 9\cdot2$ to 2 s.f. and $q = 58\cdot36$ to 4 s.f., calculate pq to a reasonable degree of accuracy.

D4 If $m = 0\cdot581$ to 3 s.f. and $n = 9\cdot0$ to 2 s.f., calculate
(a) mn (b) $\dfrac{m}{n}$ to a reasonable degree of accuracy.

D5 Electricians use the formula $I = \dfrac{V}{R}$ to calculate the current,
I amps, in a component when they know the voltage, V volts, and the resistance, R ohms.
If $V = 15\cdot4$ to 3 s.f. and $R = 0\cdot045$ to 2 s.f., calculate I to a reasonable degree of accuracy.

D6 The diameter of a circle is $2\cdot5$ metres to 2 s.f. Given that $\pi = 3\cdot141593$ to 7 s.f., calculate the circumference. Give your answer to a reasonable degree of accuracy.

D7 (a) If $a = 25$ and $b = 38$, both to 2 s.f., calculate a reasonable value for ab.
(b) Calculate the smallest and largest possible values of ab.

There is no 'rule of thumb' for adding and subtracting approximate numbers.
Generally speaking, it only makes sense to add or subtract two numbers when they are both rounded off to the nearest thousand, or nearest tenth, etc.
The number of significant figures is not the important thing.

3 Trigonometry (1)

A Sides and angles in a right-angled triangle

The word 'trigonometry' comes from Greek words meaning 'triangle measurement'. In trigonometry we study the relationships between the sides and angles of right-angled triangles. First you need to know some words which are used to describe the sides of a triangle.

Here is a triangle ABC, whose angles are 30°, 40° and 110°.
In this triangle, the side AB is **opposite** the angle of 110°,
     the side BC is **opposite** the angle of 30°,
     the side AC is **opposite** the angle of 40°.

In a right-angled triangle, the longest side is always opposite the right-angle, and is called the **hypotenuse**.

Here is a right-angled triangle PQR. The right-angle is at Q and the angle at P is 37°.

The side PR is the **hypotenuse**.
The side QR is **opposite** the angle of 37°.
We say the side PQ is **adjacent** to the angle of 37°.

('Adjacent' means 'next to'. There are in fact two sides which are next to the angle of 37°, PQ and PR.
But PR already has the special name hypotenuse, so only PQ is called the side adjacent to 37°.)

A1 For each of these right-angled triangles, write down which side is
(i) the hypotenuse (ii) opposite angle a (iii) adjacent to angle a

(a)   (b)   (c)

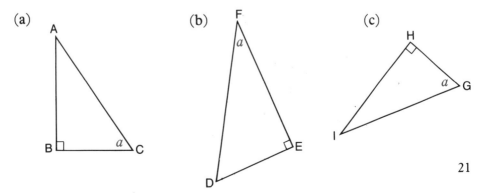

B Similar right-angled triangles

These are all right-angled triangles. Every one has an angle of 35° in it.

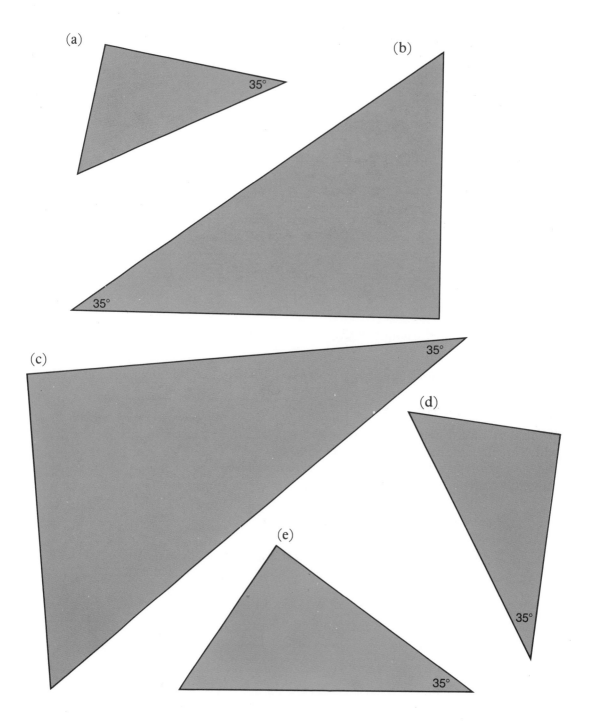

The triangles on the opposite page are all **similar** to each other.
You can see this when they are cut out and placed on top of
one another.

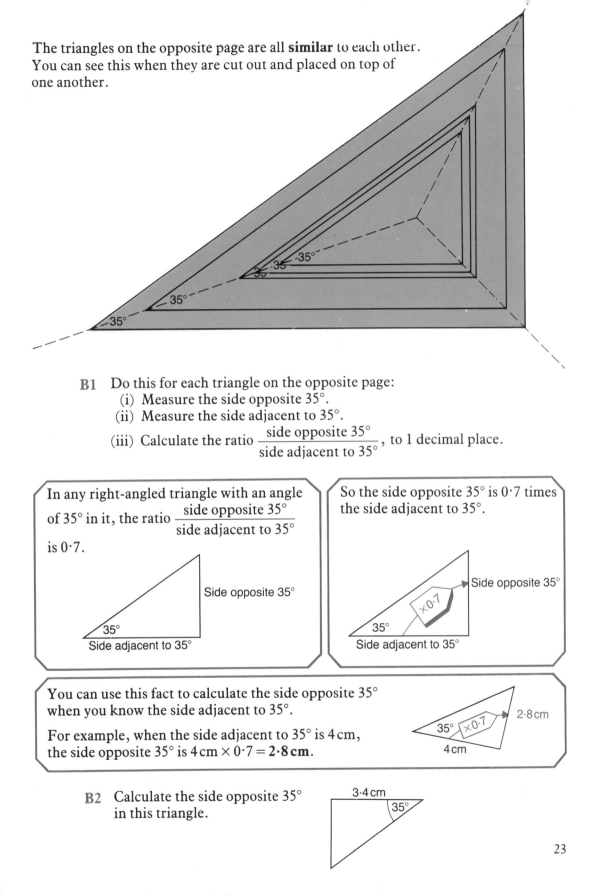

B1 Do this for each triangle on the opposite page:
  (i) Measure the side opposite 35°.
  (ii) Measure the side adjacent to 35°.
  (iii) Calculate the ratio $\dfrac{\text{side opposite } 35°}{\text{side adjacent to } 35°}$, to 1 decimal place.

In any right-angled triangle with an angle
of 35° in it, the ratio $\dfrac{\text{side opposite } 35°}{\text{side adjacent to } 35°}$
is 0·7.

Side opposite 35°

35°
Side adjacent to 35°

So the side opposite 35° is 0·7 times
the side adjacent to 35°.

×0·7

Side opposite 35°

35°
Side adjacent to 35°

You can use this fact to calculate the side opposite 35°
when you know the side adjacent to 35°.

For example, when the side adjacent to 35° is 4 cm,
the side opposite 35° is 4 cm × 0·7 = **2·8 cm**.

35° ×0·7

2·8 cm

4 cm

B2 Calculate the side opposite 35°
in this triangle.

3·4 cm

35°

23

The triangles drawn in red on this picture are all right-angled triangles.
Every one has an angle of 35° in it.

B3 Calculate the heights marked a, b, c in these diagrams.

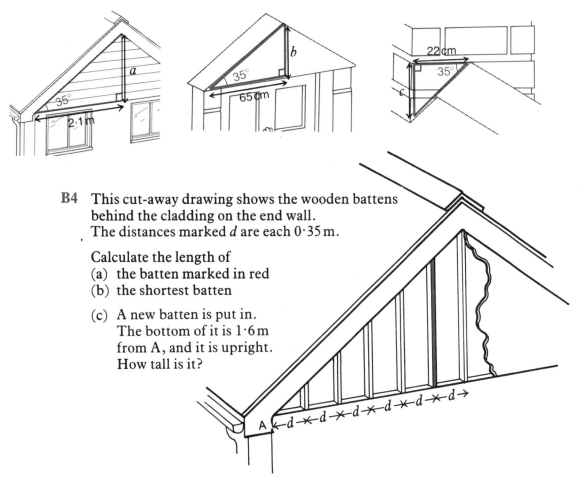

B4 This cut-away drawing shows the wooden battens behind the cladding on the end wall.
The distances marked d are each 0·35 m.

Calculate the length of
(a) the batten marked in red
(b) the shortest batten

(c) A new batten is put in. The bottom of it is 1·6 m from A, and it is upright. How tall is it?

B5 A TV aerial is erected by the dormer window. The pole is 2·1 m long. What length of pole is above the roof of the window?

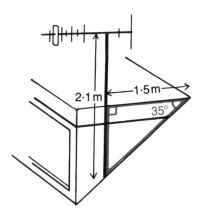

B6 The ladder reaches 4·6 m up the wall. How far is the bottom of the ladder from the wall?

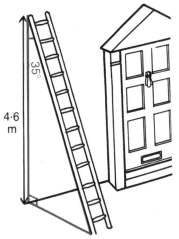

c The tangent of an angle

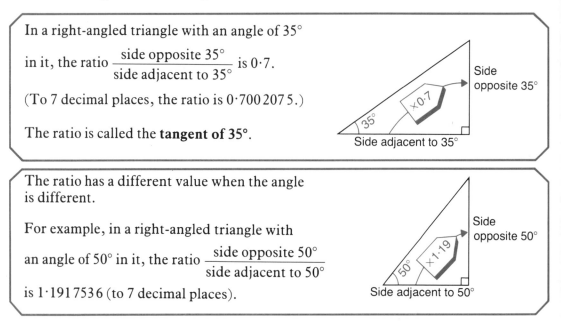

In a right-angled triangle with an angle of 35°
in it, the ratio $\dfrac{\text{side opposite 35°}}{\text{side adjacent to 35°}}$ is 0·7.

(To 7 decimal places, the ratio is 0·700 207 5.)

The ratio is called the **tangent of 35°**.

The ratio has a different value when the angle
is different.

For example, in a right-angled triangle with

an angle of 50° in it, the ratio $\dfrac{\text{side opposite 50°}}{\text{side adjacent to 50°}}$

is 1·191 7536 (to 7 decimal places).

Here is a table of some angles and their tangents. Each tangent
is given correct to 3 decimal places.

Angle	0°	5°	10°	15°	20°	25°	30°	35°	40°
Tangent	0	0·087	0·176	0·268	0·364	0·466	0·577	0·700	0·839

Angle	45°	50°	55°	60°	65°	70°	75°	80°	85°
Tangent	1	1·192	1·428	1·732	2·145	2·747	3·732	5·671	11·430

The Greek letter θ ('theta') is often used to stand for an angle.
In a right-angled triangle with an angle θ in it,

the ratio $\dfrac{\text{side opposite }\theta}{\text{side adjacent to }\theta}$ is the tangent of θ (written **tan θ** for short).

This diagram shows that you calculate the side opposite θ by
multiplying the side adjacent to θ by tan θ.

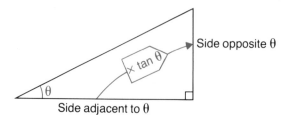

Side adjacent to θ × tan θ = side opposite θ

You may find it helpful to copy this diagram and the formula
into your book.

26

Worked example

Calculate the side opposite 20° in this triangle.

The angle of 20° is at the top of the triangle.
The side adjacent to 20° is 4·6 m long.

So 4·6 m × tan 20° = side opposite 20°.

From the table of tangents, tan 20° = 0·364,
so the side opposite 20° = 4·6 m × 0·364
$$= \textbf{1·7 m} \text{ (to 1 d.p.).}$$

C1 Calculate the lengths marked with letters in these diagrams.
Give each answer correct to the nearest 0·1 m.

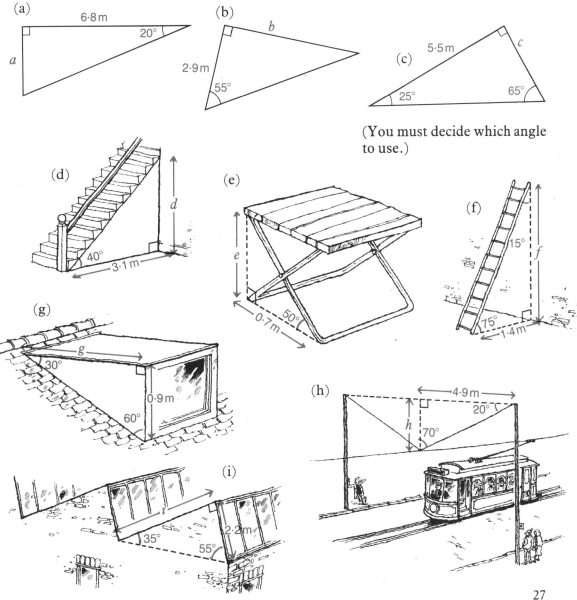

(a) 6·8 m, 20°, a

(b) b, 2·9 m, 55°

(c) 5·5 m, c, 25°, 65°

(You must decide which angle to use.)

(d) d, 40°, 3·1 m

(e) e, 0·7 m, 50°

(f) 15°, f, 75°, 1·4 m

(g) g, 30°, 0·9 m, 60°

(h) 4·9 m, 20°, h, 70°

(i) 35°, i, 2·2 m, 55°

27

D Using a calculator

On a scientific calculator you will find a key marked $\boxed{\text{tan}}$.
Before you use it, make sure the calculator is set to work in degrees.

To find tan 25°, first enter 25 and then press $\boxed{\text{tan}}$.
The calculator will give the result 0·466 307 . . . depending on how
many figures it displays.

> **D1** Use a calculator to find these.
> (a) tan 37°   (b) tan 53°   (c) tan 22·5°   (d) tan 89·9°

You can use a calculator to work out the side opposite a given angle
in a right-angled triangle, when you know the side adjacent to the angle.
In the triangle on the right,

   5·7 m × tan 23° = AB.

On most calculators you can do
5·7 × tan 23° like this:

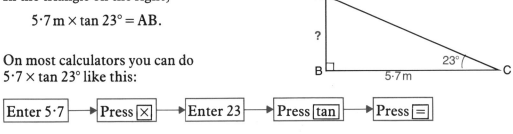

The result should be 2·419 506 . . . So AB = 2·4 m to 1 d.p.

> **D2** Calculate, correct to 1 d.p.,   (a) 4·6 × tan 54°   (b) 72·3 × tan 9°

> **D3** Calculate the sides marked with letters, to the nearest 0·1 m.

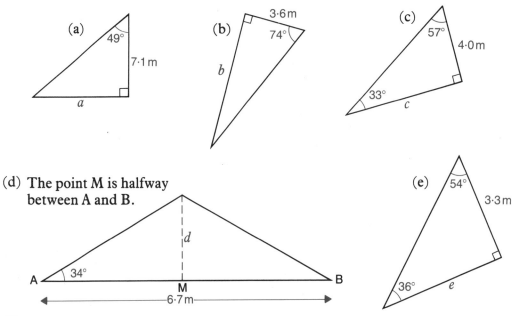

(d) The point M is halfway
   between A and B.

Calculating the side adjacent to an angle

In this triangle the side opposite 37° is 4 cm.
The side adjacent to 37° is unknown. Let it be x cm.

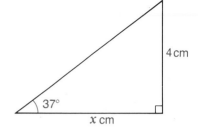

We know that $x \times \tan 37° = 4$.

Divide both sides by tan 37°: $\dfrac{x \times \tan 37°}{\tan 37°} = \dfrac{4}{\tan 37°}$

So $x = \dfrac{4}{\tan 37°}$

On most calculators you can do $4 \div \tan 37°$ like this:

Enter 4 ⟶ Press ÷ ⟶ Enter 37 ⟶ Press tan ⟶ Press =

The result should be 5·3 cm to 1 d.p.

(You can see from the rough sketch above that x must be greater than 4 cm. You can use this as a check on the result.)

> **D4** In each case below, use the formula
>
> side adjacent to $\theta \times \tan \theta$ = side opposite θ
>
> to write down an equation with the unknown side in it.
> Then solve the equation, correct to 1 d.p.
> (The first one is done as an example.)

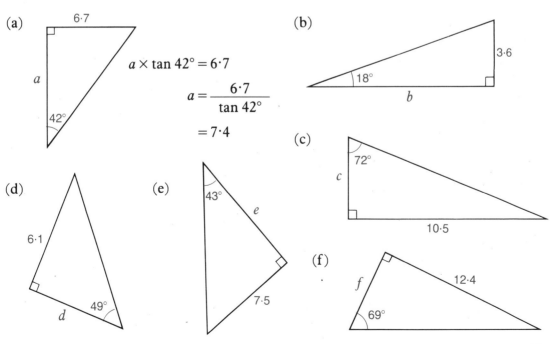

(a)

$a \times \tan 42° = 6·7$

$a = \dfrac{6·7}{\tan 42°}$

$= 7·4$

D5 Calculate the sides marked with letters in these triangles.
Be careful: sometimes the lettered side is opposite the given angle,
and sometimes it is adjacent to it.

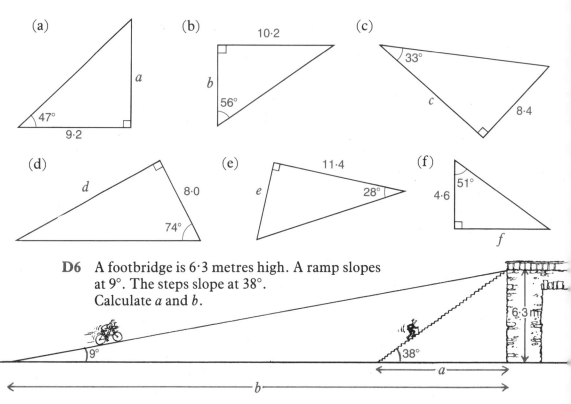

(a)

(b) 10·2

(c) 33° 8·4

(d) 8·0

(e) 11·4 28°

(f) 51° 4·6

D6 A footbridge is 6·3 metres high. A ramp slopes
at 9°. The steps slope at 38°.
Calculate a and b.

Angles of elevation

If you stand and look directly at the top of a tall tree,
your line of sight slopes upwards from the horizontal.
The angle between your line of sight and the horizontal
is called the **angle of elevation** of the top of the tree from
where you are standing.

Surveyors measure angles of elevation with an
instrument called a 'theodolite'.

D7 Suppose that the distance MH in the picture is 10 metres,
and the angle of elevation is 25°.
(a) Calculate the distance TH, to the nearest 0·1 metre.
(b) To find the height of the tree, you have to add the distance HG.
This is the same as the height of the man's eyes above the ground.
If his eyes are 1·6 m above the ground, how high is the tree?

D8 The same man stands 25 m away from a flagpole and finds that the
angle of elevation of the top of the pole is 41°. How tall is the pole?

E Inverse tangents

So far we have used tangents to solve two kinds of problem connected with right-angled triangles:
(1) calculating the side opposite an angle, when the angle and the side adjacent to it are known;
(2) calculating the side adjacent to an angle, when the angle and the side opposite it are known.

There is a third kind of problem as well:
(3) calculating an angle when the sides opposite it and adjacent to it are known.

Here is an example of this kind of problem.
θ is unknown.
The side adjacent to θ is 4 cm.
The side opposite θ is 2 cm.

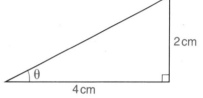

2 cm

4 cm

We know that   side adjacent to $\theta \times \tan \theta =$ side opposite θ

so it follows that $4 \times \tan \theta = 2$

Divide both sides by 4. $\dfrac{4 \times \tan \theta}{4} = \dfrac{2}{4}$

$\tan \theta = 0\cdot5$

Now we have to find the angle whose tangent is $0\cdot5$.

On a calculator we know how to start with an angle and find its tangent. Now we need to carry out the **inverse** process: starting with the tangent and finding the angle.
On many calculators there is a key marked $\boxed{\text{inv}}$ for this.
If you know the tangent is $0\cdot5$, you find the angle like this:

$$\boxed{\text{Enter } 0\cdot5} \longrightarrow \boxed{\text{Press } \boxed{\text{inv}}} \longrightarrow \boxed{\text{Press } \boxed{\text{tan}}}$$

Result **26·565 . . .**
(On some calculators instead of $\boxed{\text{inv}}$ you press $\boxed{\text{arc}}$ or $\boxed{\text{2nd F}}$.
Find out how yours works.)

The angle whose tangent is $0\cdot5$ is $26\cdot6°$ (to 1 d.p.).
We can write this in two ways.

$\tan 26\cdot6° = 0\cdot5$ inv tan $0\cdot5 = 26\cdot6°$

> **E1** Use a calculator to find (to 1 d.p.) the angle whose tangent is $0\cdot6$.

> **E2** What angles have these tangents?
>   (a) $0\cdot75$ (b) $1\cdot35$ (c) $0\cdot08$ (d) $37\cdot1$ (e) 213

31

E3 Enter 43 into your calculator, press tan and then inv tan .
You should get back to 43. Try it with other angles.

Worked example

Calculate the angle marked x in this triangle.

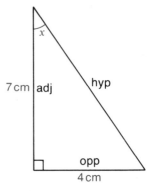

First label the sides 'hyp', 'opp' and 'adj'.

Write down the basic formula:

$$\text{adj} \times \tan x = \text{opp}$$

We get $\qquad 7 \times \tan x = 4,$

$$\tan x = \frac{4}{7}.$$

On the calculator, we do $4 \div 7$ and press = .
We get $0\cdot571\,428\ldots$ This is the value of **tan x**.

$$\tan x = 0\cdot571\,428\ldots$$

To find x we need the **inverse tangent** of $0\cdot571\,428\ldots$, or in other words the angle whose tangent is $0\cdot571\,428\ldots$

So we leave the number $0\cdot571\,428\ldots$ in the calculator and press inv tan .
We get $29\cdot7448\ldots$

$$\text{So } x = \mathbf{29\cdot7°} \text{ to 1 d.p.}$$

E4 Calculate the angles marked with letters in these triangles, to the nearest $0\cdot1°$.

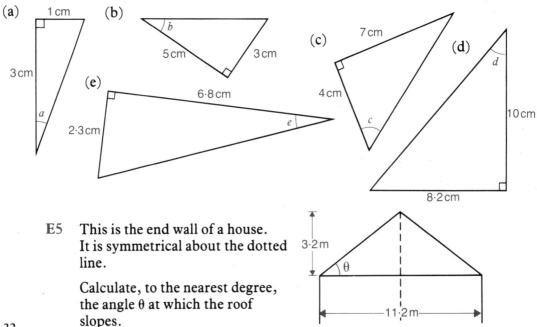

E5 This is the end wall of a house. It is symmetrical about the dotted line.

Calculate, to the nearest degree, the angle θ at which the roof slopes.

32

E6 The drawing on the right shows the end wall of a shed.

Calculate the angle which the roof makes with the horizontal (the angle marked x). Give the angle to the nearest degree.

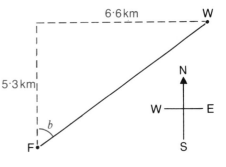

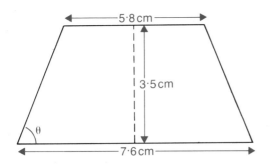

E7 The shape on the left is symmetrical about the dotted line.

Calculate the angle marked θ, to the nearest $0.1°$.

E8 A windmill W is 5.3 km north of a farmhouse F, and 6.6 km east of F.

(a) Calculate, to the nearest degree, the bearing of W from F (the angle marked b in the diagram).

(b) What is the bearing of F from W?

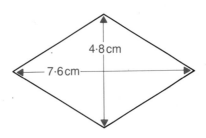

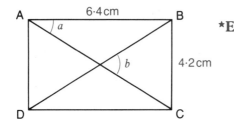

*E9 ABCD is a rectangle. Calculate
(a) the angle a between AB and AC
(b) the angle b between AC and DB

*E10 The sides of a rectangle are of lengths 13.8 cm and 10.2 cm. Calculate the angles between the diagonals of the rectangle.

*E11 The diagonals of a rhombus are 7.6 cm and 4.8 cm long.

Calculate the four angles of the rhombus.

*E12 A right-angled triangle has sides 30 cm, 40 cm and 50 cm. Calculate the angles of the triangle.

33

4 Rates

A Constant rates

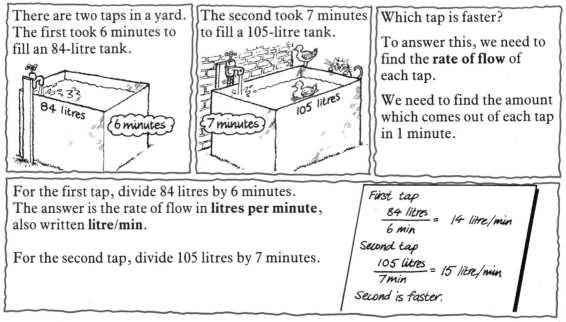

There are two taps in a yard. The first took 6 minutes to fill an 84-litre tank.

The second took 7 minutes to fill a 105-litre tank.

Which tap is faster?

To answer this, we need to find the **rate of flow** of each tap.

We need to find the amount which comes out of each tap in 1 minute.

For the first tap, divide 84 litres by 6 minutes. The answer is the rate of flow in **litres per minute**, also written **litre/min**.

For the second tap, divide 105 litres by 7 minutes.

First tap
$$\frac{84 \text{ litres}}{6 \text{ min}} = 14 \text{ litre/min}$$

Second tap
$$\frac{105 \text{ litres}}{7 \text{ min}} = 15 \text{ litre/min}$$

Second is faster.

A1 Calculate the rate of flow of these taps in litre/min, correct to the nearest whole number.
  (a) A tap which fills a 40-litre drum in 4 minutes
  (b) One which fills a 600-litre tank in 9 minutes
  (c) One which takes 17 minutes to fill a 200-litre tank
  (d) One which takes 4·5 minutes to fill a 30-litre drum

A2 A fire engine's hose delivers water at 3500 litre/min. How much water does it deliver in 15 minutes?

A3 A freshwater spring takes 7·5 minutes to fill a 2·5-litre bottle. What is the rate of flow of the spring in litre/min?

A4 Water comes out of a tap at the rate of 14 litre/min.
  (a) Copy and complete this table showing the amount of water which comes out in different times.

Time in minutes	0	0·5	1	1·5	2	3	4	5
Amount in litres	0							

  (b) Draw a graph of (time, amount).
  (c) Use the graph to find the time this tap will take to fill a tank which can hold 50 litres.

A tap whose rate of flow is constant at 20 litre/min gives a straight-line graph like this.

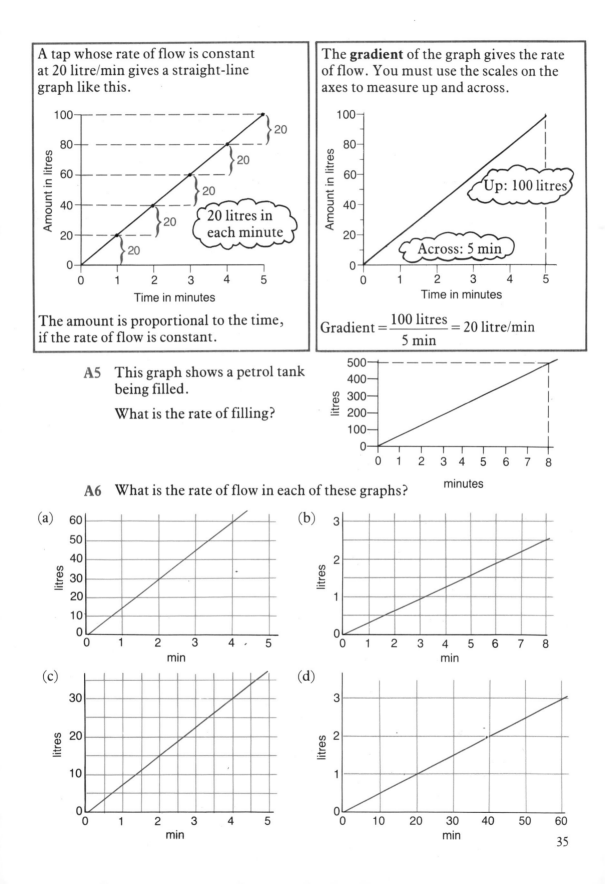

The amount is proportional to the time, if the rate of flow is constant.

The **gradient** of the graph gives the rate of flow. You must use the scales on the axes to measure up and across.

$$\text{Gradient} = \frac{100 \text{ litres}}{5 \text{ min}} = 20 \text{ litre/min}$$

A5 This graph shows a petrol tank being filled.

What is the rate of filling?

A6 What is the rate of flow in each of these graphs?

(a)

(b)

(c)

(d)

35

If you divide an amount in **litres** by an amount in **minutes**
you get a rate in **litres per minute**.

This works with other units as well.

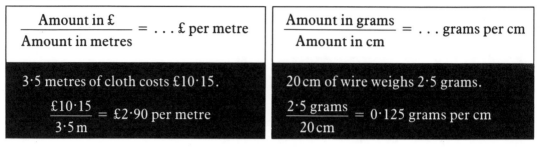

$\dfrac{\text{Amount in £}}{\text{Amount in metres}} = \dots \text{£ per metre}$	$\dfrac{\text{Amount in grams}}{\text{Amount in cm}} = \dots \text{grams per cm}$
3·5 metres of cloth costs £10·15. $\dfrac{£10·15}{3·5\,\text{m}} = £2·90 \text{ per metre}$	20 cm of wire weighs 2·5 grams. $\dfrac{2·5\,\text{grams}}{20\,\text{cm}} = 0·125 \text{ grams per cm}$

A7 An aircraft travelling at a constant speed took 23 seconds
to fly 5000 metres.
What was its speed in metres per second, to the nearest whole number?

A8 A machine making plastic tubing spews out 97·5 metres of tubing
in 15 seconds.
At what rate does the tubing come out of the machine?

A9 If £15 is worth the same as $19, work out the exchange rate.
between the pound and the dollar (to 2 d.p.)
(a) in dollars per pound   (b) in pounds per dollar

A10 A typist is paid £99 for 36 hours' work.
What is his rate of pay per hour?

A11 A girl who delivers newspapers works for $13\frac{1}{2}$ hours each week
and earns £8·50 a week.
What is her rate of pay per hour (to the nearest penny)?

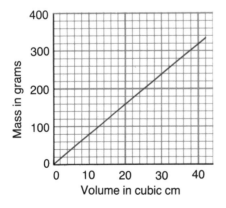

A12 This graph shows how the mass of
a piece of iron is related to its
volume.

(a) Calculate the gradient of the
graph. (Write the units correctly.)

(b) What name is given to the quantity
you have just calculated?

A13 The paper on which this book is printed is described as '50 g/m²'.
What does this mean?

B Average rates

The 16:15 train from Edinburgh to London gets to London at 21:15.
It takes 5 hours to cover the distance of 393 miles.

The train does not travel at a constant speed throughout the journey.
Sometimes it speeds up and sometimes it slows down or stops.
If we divide the total distance travelled by the total time taken, the rate
we get is called the **average speed** of the train.

$$\frac{393 \text{ miles}}{5 \text{ hours}} = 78 \cdot 6 \text{ miles per hour (average speed)}$$

B1 In 1960, the 'Flying Scotsman' took 7 hours to go from London to
Edinburgh. What was its average speed?

B2 Calculate the average speed of a train which travels from
London to Penzance (305 miles) in 6·4 hours.

To calculate a speed in m.p.h. you divide the distance in miles by the time
in hours. If the time is given in hours and minutes, you have to change
the minutes to a decimal of an hour, using the fact that 1 minute = $\frac{1}{60}$ hour.

For example, 13 minutes = $\frac{13}{60}$ hour $(= 13 \div 60)$ = 0·22 hour, to 2 d.p.

B3 Write these in hours, to 2 d.p.
(a) 47 minutes   (b) 6 hours 28 minutes   (c) 2 hours 7 minutes

B4 From London to Liverpool is 193·5 miles. The 11:50 train from
London gets to Liverpool at 14:28. Calculate its average speed.

The average rate of fuel consumption of a car is measured in **litres per 100 km**.
To calculate it you divide the amount of fuel used, in litres, by the
number of **hundreds** of kilometres travelled.

So if a car uses up 13 litres of fuel in travelling 142 km,

$$\text{average fuel consumption rate} = \frac{13 \text{ litres}}{1 \cdot 42 \text{ hundred km}} = 9 \cdot 15 \text{ litre/100 km}$$

B5 What is the average fuel consumption rate of a car which travels
263 km on 30 litres of fuel?

B6 Calculate the average fuel consumption rate of a van which
uses 34·6 litres of petrol to travel 180 km.

B7 (a) If 142 km = 1·42 hundred km, what is 86 km in hundred km?
(b) Calculate the average fuel consumption rate of a car
which travels 86 km on 10 litres of petrol.
(c) Calculate the average fuel consumption rate of a car
which uses 5·3 litres of petrol to travel 58 km.

C Changes in rates

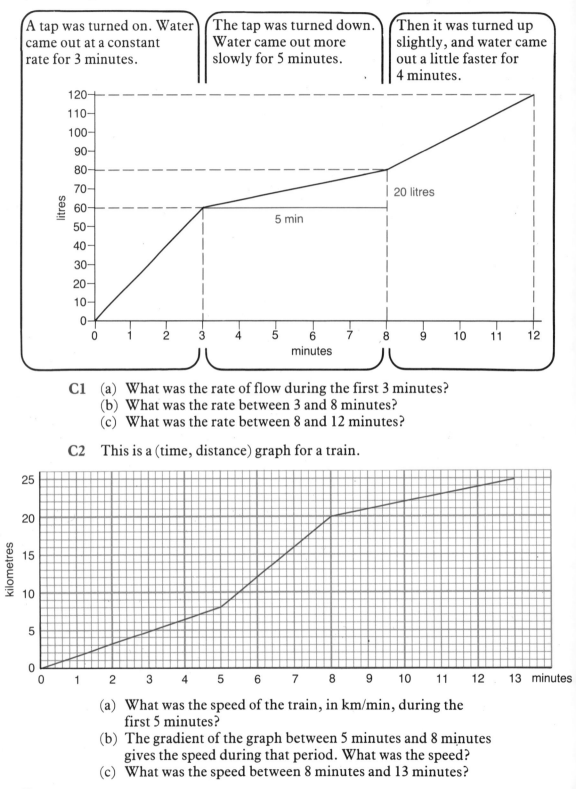

| A tap was turned on. Water came out at a constant rate for 3 minutes. | The tap was turned down. Water came out more slowly for 5 minutes. | Then it was turned up slightly, and water came out a little faster for 4 minutes. |

C1 (a) What was the rate of flow during the first 3 minutes?
(b) What was the rate between 3 and 8 minutes?
(c) What was the rate between 8 and 12 minutes?

C2 This is a (time, distance) graph for a train.

(a) What was the speed of the train, in km/min, during the first 5 minutes?
(b) The gradient of the graph between 5 minutes and 8 minutes gives the speed during that period. What was the speed?
(c) What was the speed between 8 minutes and 13 minutes?

C3 This is a (time, distance) graph for an aircraft.

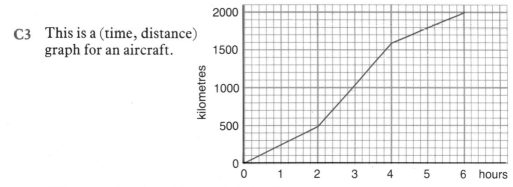

What was the aircraft's speed, in km/h,
(a) from 0 to 2 hours   (b) from 2 to 4 hours   (c) from 4 to 6 hours

The aircraft in question C3 travelled a total distance of 2000 km in a total time of 6 hours.

So its average speed for the whole journey is $\dfrac{2000}{6} = 333$ km/h (to the nearest km/h).

The average speed is the gradient of the dotted line.

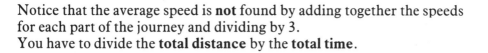

Notice that the average speed is **not** found by adding together the speeds for each part of the journey and dividing by 3.
You have to divide the **total distance** by the **total time**.

C4 Calculate the average speed (to the nearest $0 \cdot 1$ km/min) of the train whose (time, distance) graph is given in question C2.

C5 A car travels at 20 km per hour for 3 hours, and then at 30 km per hour for 4 hours.
(a) How far does it travel altogether?
(b) How many hours does it take for the whole journey?
(c) What is its average speed for the journey?

C6 A train leaves A at 08:00. The map on the left shows when it gets to other stations, and the distance of each station from A.

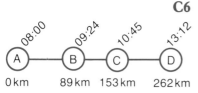

Calculate the average speed of the train between
(a) A and B   (b) B and C   (c) C and D   (d) A and D

39

Some water was heated. This graph shows how its temperature went up.

In the period between 0 and 2 minutes from the start, the temperature went up from 8 °C to 22 °C.

So in that period the temperature rose by 14 degrees in 2 minutes.

So the average rate of increase of the temperature **during that period** was $\dfrac{14 \text{ degrees}}{2 \text{ min}}$
$= 7$ degrees/min.

This means that if the temperature had continued to rise at the same rate, it would have risen 7 degrees in each minute afterwards.
But as you can see from the graph, it only rose by 9 degrees between 2 min and 4 min. So in this period the average rate of increase was $\dfrac{9 \text{ degrees}}{2 \text{ min}} = 4{\cdot}5$ degrees/min.

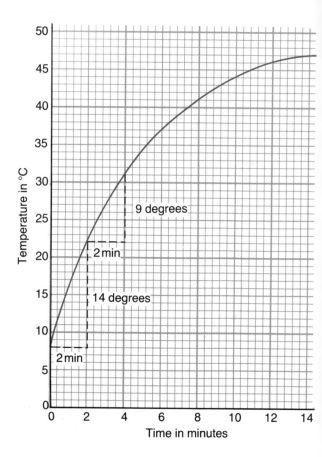

The rate of increase in 'degrees per minute' decreases as time goes on.
The temperature continues to go up, but it goes up more and more slowly.

C7 What was the average rate of increase of the temperature, in degrees per minute, in the period between
(a) 4 min and 6 min   (b) 6 min and 8 min   (c) 8 min and 10 min
(d) 10 min and 12 min   (e) 12 min and 14 min

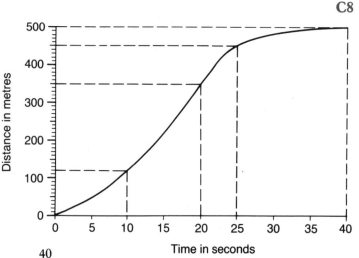

C8 This is the (time, distance) graph for a tramcar travelling between two stops 500 metres apart.

(a) How far did the tramcar go between 0 sec and 10 sec?
(b) What was its average speed in m/s during that period?
(c) What was its average speed
   (i) between 10 sec and 20 sec
   (ii) between 20 sec and 25 sec
   (iii) between 25 sec and 40 sec
(d) What was its overall average speed for the whole journey?

40

C9 Some liquid is heated and then left to cool.
    This graph shows how its temperature changes.

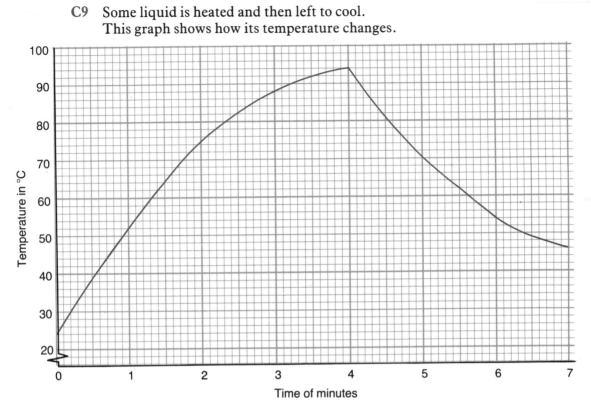

(a) What was the average rate of increase of temperature in
    degrees per minute between
    (i) 0 min and 1·5 min   (ii) 1·5 min and 2 min   (iii) 2 min and 4 min?
(b) What was the average rate of decrease of temperature between
    (i) 4 min and 5 min   (ii) 5 min and 5·5 min   (iii) 5·5 min and 7 min?

D Calculations with rates

To find a rate in **litres per minute** you divide an amount in **litres** by
an amount in **minutes**. For example, $\dfrac{18\ \text{litres}}{3\ \text{min}} = 6$ **litre/min**.

There are two other types of calculation with rates. Here are examples.

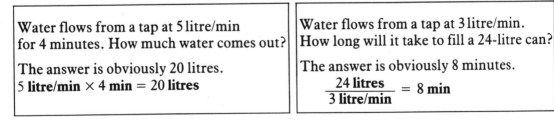

Water flows from a tap at 5 litre/min for 4 minutes. How much water comes out?	Water flows from a tap at 3 litre/min. How long will it take to fill a 24-litre can?
The answer is obviously 20 litres.	The answer is obviously 8 minutes.
5 **litre/min** × 4 **min** = 20 **litres**	$\dfrac{24\ \textbf{litres}}{3\ \textbf{litre/min}} = 8$ **min**

D1 A tap flows at 6 litre/min.
    (a) How long will it take to fill a 54-litre tank?
    (b) How much water comes out of the tap in $4\frac{1}{2}$ minutes?

41

Look carefully at the **pattern** of units.

$$\frac{10 \text{ litres}}{2 \text{ min}} = 5 \text{ litre/min}$$

$$3 \text{ litre/min} \times 4 \text{ min} = 12 \text{ litres}$$

$$\frac{18 \text{ litres}}{6 \text{ litre/min}} = 3 \text{ min}$$

The same pattern works with any units.

$$\frac{\ldots \text{ miles}}{\ldots \text{ hours}} = \ldots \text{ mile/hour}$$

$$\ldots \text{ deg/min} \times \ldots \text{ min} = \ldots \text{ deg}$$

$$\frac{\ldots \text{ m}}{\ldots \text{ m/s}} = \ldots \text{ s}$$

D2 How long does it take to travel 156 miles at a speed of 24 m.p.h.?

D3 How long does it take to fill a 34 000-gallon petrol tank at a rate of 8500 gallons per hour?

D4 A sugar solution contains 72·5 g of sugar per litre.
(a) How much sugar is there in 0·80 litre of solution?
(b) How many litres of solution will contain 16 g of sugar?
(Give your answer correct to the nearest 0·01 litre.)

D5 The electrical resistance of a type of wire is 0·45 ohms per metre. How many metres of the wire will have a resistance of 63 ohms?

D6 The volume of water in a reservoir has gone down from 18 200 cubic metres to 13 900 cubic metres during the last 7 days.
(a) What is the average rate at which the water has been used, in cubic metres per day (correct to the nearest 100)?
(b) If the water continues to be used up at the same rate, after how many more days will the reservoir be empty?

D7 If a person's heart beats at an average rate of 60 beats per minute, how many times does it beat in a lifetime of 70 years? (Write your answer in standard index form, to 1 s.f.)

D8 A nurse takes 0·6 litre of a solution containing 80 g of glucose per litre, and mixes it with 1·9 litres of a solution containing 150 g of glucose per litre.

Calculate the number of grams of glucose per litre of the mixture.

D9 A car travelling at 60 km/hour uses up petrol at a rate of 8 litres/100 km.
Calculate the rate of petrol consumption in litres per hour.

D10 A bath can hold 600 litres of water. If it is filled from the cold tap, it takes $2\frac{1}{2}$ minutes to fill. If it is filled from the hot tap, it takes 3 minutes.
How long does it take to fill when both taps are on?

5 Algebraic expressions

A Terms

Look at the expression on the right. It consists of 'bits' with + signs between them. Each bit is called a **term** of the expression. So this expression has four terms.	$3a + 5b + 4a + b$
Adding in a different order does not change the result. So we can re-write the expression like this.	$3a + 4a + 5b + b$

$3a + 4a$ can be replaced by $7a$ (just as
3 sixes + 4 sixes = 7 sixes).
$5b + b$ can be replaced by $6b$ (because
b means the same as $1b$).
Now there are only two terms.
The original expression has been **simplified**.

$$7a \quad + \quad 6b$$

The terms $3a$ and $4a$ are called **like terms**. They can be replaced by
a single term. Similarly, $5b$ and b are like terms.
But $7a$ and $6b$ are **unlike terms**. You cannot replace $7a + 6b$ by
a single term. So the expression above cannot be simplified any further.

> **A1** Simplify each of these expressions as far as possible.
> (Some of them cannot be simplified.)
> (a) $a + 3b + 5b + 4a$ (b) $2p + 3q + 8p + q$ (c) $x + 2y + 3z + x$
> (d) $4h + 3k + 2l$ (e) $s + t + 3t + s$ (f) $4m + 4n + 7p + q$

In the expression $4a + 3 + 5a + 1$, the terms $4a$ and $5a$ are like terms,
and the terms 3 and 1 are like terms. So the expression can be simplified
to $9a + 4$.

> **A2** Simplify these expressions where possible.
> (a) $3x + 2 + 5 + 8x$ (b) $6p + 5q + 3 + 6$ (c) $2a + 3b + 5c + 6$
> (d) $5s + t + s + 5$ (e) $7 + 3y + 2 + 4y$ (f) $8x + 3 + 2x + 1$

In the expression $a^2 + a$, **the terms a^2 and a are unlike terms.**
You cannot replace $a^2 + a$ by a single term.
(You can replace $a^2 \times a$ by a^3, but you cannot replace $a^2 + a$.)

In the expression $3a^2 + 4a + 2a^2 + 7a$, the terms $3a^2$ and $2a^2$ are like terms,
and the terms $4a$ and $7a$ are like terms. So the expression can be simplified
to $5a^2 + 11a$, but no further.

> **A3** Simplify   (a) $3x^2 + 2x + 5x^2 + x$ (b) $6y + y^2 + 3y + 7y^2$

In the expression $a + ab$, **the terms a and ab are unlike terms.**
You cannot replace $a + ab$ by a single term.
(You can replace $a \times ab$ by a^2b, but you cannot replace $a + ab$.)

Similarly, in the expression $a^2 + ab$, **the terms a^2 and ab are unlike.**
(You can replace $a^2 \times ab$ by a^3b, but you cannot replace $a^2 + ab$.)

The general rule for like terms is this:

Like terms are exactly alike except for the **number** in them.

For example: $3ab, 5ab, 6ab, ab$ (or $1ab$) are all like terms.
$6x^2, 3x^2, 20x^2, 5x^2, x^2$ are all like terms.
$p, 3p, 7p, 38p, 204p$ are all like terms.

Worked example

Simplify the expression $2a^2 + 3ab + 4a + 5a^2 + 4ab + 16$.

The only groups of like terms are $2a^2, 5a^2$ and $3ab, 4ab$.
The expression can be re-written in this order: $2a^2 + 5a^2 + 3ab + 4ab + 4a + 16$.

Now it can be simplified to four terms like this: $7a^2 \quad + \quad 7ab \quad + 4a + 16$.

A4 Simplify these expressions as far as possible.
(Some of them cannot be simplified.)
(a) $6x + 3x + 2x^2 + 5x^2$
(b) $3p + 5pq + 2q + 2pq + 4p$
(c) $a^2 + 2a + b^2 + 3ab$
(d) $4m^2 + 2n^2 + 5mn + n^2 + 3m$
(e) $3f^2 + 5f + f^2 + f$
(f) $st + t + 3s + 5t + 8st$
(g) $u + 3v + 8uv + 4u$
(h) $2a^2 + 4a + 7a^2 + 6a + a^2$

Expressions with subtractions in them

The expression $3a - ab + 4b - 2a + 3ab$ can be re-written with the terms in
a different order. But when you do this you must remember that the $+$ or $-$ sign
in front of each term belongs with that term. So **each sign must go with its term**.

Here is one way of re-ordering the terms so
that like terms are together.

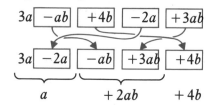

Like terms can now be replaced by a single term. $a \qquad + 2ab \qquad + 4b$

A5 Simplify these expressions where possible.
(a) $4p - 2q + 7p + 3q + 6p$
(b) $2a + 3b - 5a + 4b + a$
(c) $2x^2 + 5x - x^2 - 4x + 3x^2$
(d) $xy - 3x + 5y + 3xy - 2x$
(e) $p^2 + pq - q^2 - 6pq - 2q$
(f) $3a + 5b - 4a - 6b - 5a$
(g) $4s - t + 7st - 2t - s$
(h) $8mn - 3m - 2n - 5m - 6n$
(i) $u^2 - v^2 + 2uv - 3u - v$
(j) $2r^2 - 5s^2 + 7rs + r^2 + s^2$.
(k) $ab + a - 2ab - 3a - b$
(l) $2x^2 - 3xy - 5x^2 - xy - x^2$
(m) $pq - p - q + 4p - 5pq$
(n) $e^2 - 2f^2 - 4ef + 7f^2 - 3e^2$

B Brackets (1)

Suppose you go into a shop with 90p. You buy a book for 40p and a
pen for 20p. There are two ways of calculating what you have left.

1 The total amount spent is $40 + 20$.
So you subtract this total from 90.

$$90 - (40 + 20)$$

2 Start with 90. First subtract the 40,
then subtract the 20.

$$90 - 40 - 20$$

Both methods obviously lead to the same answer, but one calculation has
brackets in it and the other does not.

You can replace $-(40 + 20)$ by $-40 - 20$ without making any difference
to the result.

There is nothing special about the numbers: it is the pattern which is important.
For example: $-(a + b)$ is equivalent to $-a - b$,
$-(x + 3)$ is equivalent to $-x - 3$,
$-(s + t + u)$ is equivalent to $-s - t - u$.

B1 Write these expressions without brackets.
(a) $a - (b + c)$ (b) $p - (q + r)$ (c) $x - (3 + y)$ (d) $10 - (s + 2t)$

B2 Remove the brackets from these expressions and simplify.
The first is done as an example.

(a) $8x - (y + 2x)$ (b) $5a - (2a + b)$ (c) $3p - (p + 2q)$

$= 8x - y - 2x$ (d) $7r - (r + s)$ (e) $5u - (3v + 2u)$

$= 8x - 2x - y$ (f) $4x - (2y + x)$ (g) $a - (b + a)$

$= \quad 6x \quad - y$ (h) $2h - (3k + 4h)$ (i) $p - (4p + 8q)$

Ken has £27. He is buying a toaster. He thinks it costs £13.

I'll work out what I will have left over.

$27 - 13$

But there's £1 off the price this week.
So subtract 1 less than 13.

$27 - 13$
$27 - (13 - 1)$

The answer to $27 - (13 - 1)$ is 1 more than the answer to $27 - 13$.
So $27 - (13 - 1) = 27 - 13 + 1$.

B3 Put the signs ($+$ or $-$) in these to make the calculations correct.
(a) $7 - (3 - 1) = 7 \ldots 3 \ldots 1$ (b) $12 - (8 - 2) = 12 \ldots 8 \ldots 2$
(c) $10 - (6 - 2) = 10 \ldots 6 \ldots 2$ (d) $13 - (9 - 4) = 13 \ldots 9 \ldots 4$
(e) $5 - (7 - 6) = 5 \ldots 7 \ldots 6$ (f) $14 - (2 - 8) = 14 \ldots 2 \ldots 8$
(g) $10 - (8 - 2 - 1) = 10 \ldots 8 \ldots 2 \ldots 1$
(h) $20 - (9 - 3 - 2) = 20 \ldots 9 \ldots 3 \ldots 2$

First rule of signs for removing brackets

When you remove the brackets from $-(a+b)$ you get $-a-b$.
When you remove the brackets from $-(a-b)$ you get $-a+b$.

When you remove brackets, a 'subtract' sign in front of the brackets changes the operations inside the brackets (from 'add' to 'subtract' and vice versa).

$$-(a-b+c-d)$$
$$-a+b-c+d$$

> **Note.** A **negative** sign attached to a number or a letter does not change. Only the **operations** 'add' and 'subtract' are changed.
>
> $$-(a+\,^-b+\,^-3-d)$$
> $$-a-\,^-b-\,^-3+d$$

B4 Remove the brackets from these expressions.
  (a) $p-(q-r-s)$ (b) $a-(b+c-d)$ (c) $e-(f-g+h)$
  (d) $4a-(2b-3c)$ (e) $2p-(q+3r)$ (f) $5x-(2y-z)$
  (g) $6p-2q-(4r-s+t)$ (h) $5a+2b-(c+2d+3e)$

B5 Remove the brackets from these, and simplify if possible.
  (a) $3x-(2-4x)$ (b) $4a-(2a-b)$ (c) $5p-(2q-3p)$
  (d) $6s-(2t-s)$ (e) $7u-(3-2u)$ (f) $10a-(4a-5)$
  (g) $5u-(2u+v)-(u-3v)$ (h) $8x-(2x-5)-(2-4x)$

Now we see what happens when there is a + sign in front of the brackets.

B6 Put the correct signs ($+$ or $-$) in these.
  (a) $3+(5+2)=3\ldots5\ldots2$ (b) $10+(6-1)=10\ldots6\ldots1$
  (c) $4+(7-5)=4\ldots7\ldots5$ (d) $6+(2-5)=6\ldots2\ldots5$
  (e) $7+(3+2+4+5)=7\ldots3\ldots2\ldots4\ldots5$
  (f) $8+(5-1+3-2)=8\ldots5\ldots1\ldots3\ldots2$

Second rule of signs for removing brackets

When you remove brackets, an 'add' sign in front of the brackets does not change the operations inside the brackets.

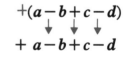

$$+(a-b+c-d)$$
$$+a-b+c-d$$

B7 Remove the brackets from these expressions.
  (a) $p+(q-r-s)$ (b) $a+(b+c-d)$ (c) $e+(f-g+h)$
  (d) $4a+(2b-3c)$ (e) $2p+(q+3r)$ (f) $5x+(2y-z)$
  (g) $6p-2q+(4r-s+t)$ (h) $5a+2b+(c-2d+3e)$

B8 Remove the brackets from these, and simplify if possible
  (a) $3x+(2-x)$ (b) $4a+(2a-b)$ (c) $5p+(2q-3p)$
  (d) $6s+(2t-s)$ (e) $2u+(3-7u)$ (f) $10a+(4a-5)$
  (g) $5u+(2u+v)-(u-3v)$ (h) $8x-(2x-5)+(2-4x)$

C Brackets (2)

You have already met expressions like $3(a + 2)$.
When you multiply out, the number in front of the brackets
multiplies each term inside. So $3(a + 2) = 3a + 6$.
Similarly $a(5 - 2b) = 5a - 2ab$.

C1 Multiply out these expressions.
(a) $2(p + q)$ (b) $2(p - q)$ (c) $3(a - 2)$ (d) $4(5 + s)$
(e) $x(3 + y)$ (f) $a(3b + 2)$ (g) $p(5 - 2q)$ (h) $r(s - t)$

You have to do two things when you multiply out the brackets in an
expression of this kind: $5c - 3(a - 2 + b)$.
(1) You have to think about the effect of the 3 in front of the brackets.
(2) You have to follow the rules of signs for the $-$ in front of the 3.

A good way to think it out in two steps is this:

1 Use the 3 to multiply the terms inside the brackets, but leave out all signs.	$5c - 3(a - 2 + b)$ $5c \quad 3a \quad 6 \quad 3b$
2 Now use the rules of signs to put the correct signs in.	$5c - 3a + 6 - 3b$

C2 Multiply out the brackets in these expressions.
(a) $4a - 2(b + 3c - 5)$ (b) $6x - 3(2y - 4z + 2)$
(c) $10s - 4(t + u + v)$ (d) $5a - 8(1 - b - 2c)$
(e) $6p - 3(2q - 4 + 3r)$ (f) $4a - b(2 - 3a + c)$
(g) $5p + p(3q - r - 2s)$ (h) $7x - 3y(x - y + 2)$

C3 Multiply out the brackets in these expressions.
Then simplify as far as possible.
The first one is done as an example.
(a) $8p - 2(3q - 4p)$ (b) $5a - 3(a + b)$
$= 8p - 6q + 8p$ (c) $5x + 2(4 - 5x)$
$= 8p + 8p - 6q$ (d) $10s - 4(2t - s)$
$= \quad 16p \quad - 6q$ (e) $9p - 5(2q - 3p)$

C4 Multiply out and simplify these if possible.
(a) $10x + 2(x - 3) - 3(x - 4)$ (b) $5a - 2(6 - 3a) + 4(2 + a)$
(c) $4ab + a(3 - b) + b(a - 4)$ (d) $2pq - p(2 - 3q) - q(3p + 1)$
(e) $13s - 5(2s - 4) + 2(3s + 1)$ (f) $3x^2 + x(2x + 1) + 4(2x + 5)$
(g) $7x^2 - 3(2x - 5) - 2x(x - 4)$ (h) $x(2x - 5) - 3(5x^2 - 2x + 4)$
(i) $p(p - q) - q(p - q)$ (j) $a(3a - 2) - b(5a + 1) - 2(a + 3)$
(k) $3s(s - t + 2) - 5t(t - 2s)$ (l) $4x - 2y - 3(x - 2y + 5)$

D Brackets (3)

You can multiply out an expression such as $(x + 2)(y + 5)$ by making a table.

	y	5
x	xy	$5x$
2	$2y$	10

So $(x + 2)(y + 5) = xy + 5x + 2y + 10$.

In the case of the expression $(x - 2)(y - 5)$, you can think of it as $(x + {}^-2)(y + {}^-5)$. The table looks like this.

	y	$^-5$
x	xy	^-5x
$^-2$	^-2y	10

$^-2 \times {}^-5 = 10$

So $(x - 2)(y - 5) = xy + {}^-5x + {}^-2y + 10$
$\qquad\qquad\quad = xy - 5x - 2y + 10$

D1 (a) Copy and complete this table for $(x + 3)(y - 4)$.

(b) Multiply out $(x + 3)(y - 4)$.

	y	$^-4$
x		
3		

D2 Make tables for these expressions, and multiply them out.

(a) $(a - 2)(b - 5)$ (b) $(s - 5)(t + 4)$ (c) $(p - 4)(q - 6)$

(d) $(x + 3)(y - 7)$ (e) $(f - 2)(g - 2)$ (f) $(m + 1)(m - 6)$

Worked examples

(1) Multiply out $(x - 3)(x + 8)$.

The table is

	x	8
x	x^2	$8x$
$^-3$	^-3x	$^-24$

$(x - 3)(x + 8) = x^2 + 8x + {}^-3x + {}^-24$
$\qquad\qquad\quad = x^2 + 8x - 3x \quad\; - 24$
$\qquad\qquad\quad = x^2 \quad\;\; + 5x \quad\;\; - 24$

(2) Multiply out $(2x - 3)(3x - 5)$.

The table is

	$3x$	$^-5$
$2x$	$6x^2$	^-10x
$^-3$	^-9x	15

$(2x - 3)(3x - 5) = 6x^2 + {}^-10x + {}^-9x + 15$
$\qquad\qquad\qquad\; = 6x^2 - 10x - 9x \quad\; + 15$
$\qquad\qquad\qquad\; = 6x^2 \quad\; - 19x \quad\;\; + 15$

D3 Multiply out each of these by making a table.

(a) $(x - 2)(x + 5)$ (b) $(a - 3)(a - 4)$ (c) $(p - 6)(p + 3)$

(d) $(2y - 1)(y + 3)$ (e) $(3q + 2)(q - 4)$ (f) $(4x - 3)(2x - 3)$

(g) $(3a - 5)(3a + 2)$ (h) $(5p - 1)(4p + 3)$ (i) $(6q - 5)(5q - 4)$

D4 Multiply out $(2x - 3)^2$.
(Remember that $(2x - 3)^2$ means $(2x - 3)(2x - 3)$.)

D5 Multiply out   (a) $(2x - 5)^2$ (b) $(3a - 4)^2$ (c) $(5p - 2)^2$

D6 Multiply out each of these expressions.

(a) $(a - 5)(2a - 3)$ (b) $(3b + 1)^2$ (c) $(3c - 2)(3c + 2)$

(d) $(4d - 5)^2$ (e) $(3x - 1)(2y - 5)$ (f) $(3f - 2)^2$

E Factorising

A large part of the art of algebra is to be able to re-write expressions in different ways. In the course of a problem, an expression may have to be re-written several times (without changing its value).

We have seen how to multiply out an expression like $3(5a + 2b)$.
The expression $3(5a + 2b)$ is written as the product of two factors, 3 and $(5a + 2b)$
We multiply the two factors together and get $15a + 6b$.

Sometimes it is necessary to go the other way and re-write an expression as the product of factors.
Starting with $15a + 6b$, we would notice that $15a$ and $6b$ are both divisible by 3.
So if we 'take out' 3 as one factor, then we have to write in brackets whatever is needed to make the result equal to $15a + 6b$.

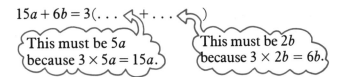

$$15a + 6b = 3(\ldots + \ldots)$$

This must be $5a$ because $3 \times 5a = 15a$.

This must be $2b$ because $3 \times 2b = 6b$.

E1 Copy and complete these.
  (a) $4a + 6b = 2(\ldots + \ldots)$ (b) $10a - 25b = 5(\ldots - \ldots)$
  (c) $12p + 16q = 4(\qquad)$ (d) $9x - 15 = 3(\qquad)$
  (e) $35s - 28t = 7(\qquad)$ (f) $18y - 6z = 6(\qquad)$

E2 Factorise these expressions. 'Take out' the largest number factor you can, and write the other factor in brackets.
  (a) $6p + 9q$ (b) $14a - 35b$ (c) $8s - 12t$ (d) $3f - 30$
  (e) $18 - 4q$ (f) $25x - 40y$ (g) $4 - 16p$ (h) $20 - 5q$

The factor outside the brackets can be a letter.
For example, in the expression $ab + 3a$ we can 'take out' a as one factor.
So $ab + 3a = a(\ldots + \ldots)$

This must be b.

This must be 3.

E3 Copy and complete these.
  (a) $2r + rs = r(\ldots + \ldots)$ (b) $3ab + b^2 = b(\ldots + \ldots)$
  (c) $4y^2 - xy = y(\qquad)$ (d) $2pq - p^2 = p(\qquad)$

E4 Factorise (a) $6pq + 5q$ (b) $6pq + 5q^2$ (c) $6pq - 5q^2$ (d) $2a^2 - 9ab$
  (e) $5a^2 - 3a$ (f) $3ab + 7b$ (g) $xy - 3y^2$ (h) $2xy + 3yz$

In the expression $4a + 6ab$ we can 'take out' $2a$ as one factor.
So $4a + 6ab = 2a(\ldots + \ldots)$

This must be 2.

This must be $3b$.

E5 Factorise (a) $8ab + 12b$ (b) $8ab + 12b^2$ (c) $8ab - 12b^2$ (d) $9a^2 - 12ab$
  (e) $5a^2 - 30a$ (f) $16xy - 12y^2$ (g) $10a^2 - 8ab$ (h) $6a^2b + 8ab^2$

1 Relationships

1.1 A van hire company charges £30 for hiring a van for up to 24 hours. Every additional 24 hours or part of 24 hours costs an extra £18.

Draw a graph of (number of hours, cost of hire) for hiring times from 0 up to 120 hours (5 days).

1.2 A student was doing experiments with a pendulum.

(a) In the first experiment she hung a mass of 50 g on the end of the pendulum. She found out how long the pendulum took to swing 20 times. Then she varied the length of the pendulum. For each different length she found out the time for 20 swings.

She made a graph and it had this shape.

Is the time for 20 swings proportional to the length of pendulum? Give the reason for your answer.

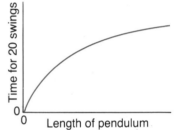

(b) In her second experiment the student kept the length the same but varied the mass on the end of the pendulum.

This time she got a graph like this.

What does the graph tell you about the time for 20 swings and the mass on the end of the pendulum?

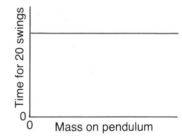

1.3 Draw graphs from the tables below. (You can use the same pair of axes for all the graphs: p from 0 to 50, q from 0 to 60.)

(a) In which case(s) is the relationship between q and p linear?

(b) In which case(s) is q proportional to p?

(1)

p	10	25	35	40
q	12	30	42	48

(2)

p	5	20	30	50
q	50	44	40	32

(3)

p	5	15	30	50
q	25	30	35	40

(4)

p	10	20	35	50
q	10	16	25	34

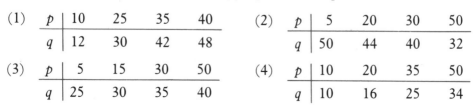

2 Accuracy

2.1 A, B and C are three stations on a railway line.
The distance from A to B is known to be between 145 and 150 km. The distance from A to C is known to be between 260 and 265 km.
Write down an interval approximation for the distance from B to C.

2.2 Write each of these as an interval approximation.
(a) 5·7 cm to 1 d.p. (b) 68·4 km to 3 s.f. (c) 5·0 g to 2 s.f.
(d) 12 800 to 3 s.f. (e) 0·0458 to 3 s.f. (f) 0·0030 to 2 s.f.

2.3 The density of a substance is found by weighing some of it and then dividing the mass by the volume. If the mass is measured in grams and the volume in cm³, the density will be in g/cm³.

The volume of a piece of aluminium is 26·4 cm³, correct to the nearest 0·1 cm³. Its mass is 71·3 g, correct to the nearest 0·1 g.

(a) Calculate the greatest and smallest possible values of the density of aluminium, based on these measurements.
(b) Give a reasonable rounded off value for the density.

2.4 The circumference of a circle is 30·6 cm to 3 s.f. Given that $\pi = 3·141593$ to 7 s.f., calculate the diameter of the circle. Give your answer to a reasonable degree of accuracy.

3 Trigonometry (1)

3.1 Calculate the sides marked with letters, to the nearest 0·1 cm.

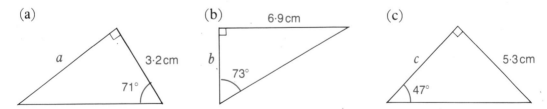

(a)   (b) 6·9 cm   (c)

3.2 Calculate the angles marked with letters, to the nearest degree.

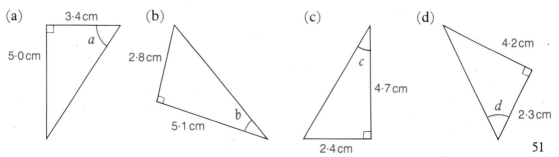

(a) 3·4 cm   (b)   (c)   (d)

51

3.3 (a) Calculate the height of an equilateral triangle whose sides are each 5 cm long, correct to the nearest 0·1 cm.

(b) Calculate the area of the triangle, to the nearest 0·1 cm².

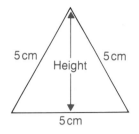
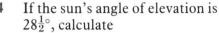

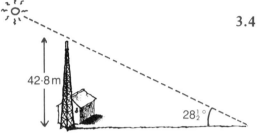

3.4 If the sun's angle of elevation is $28\frac{1}{2}°$, calculate

(a) the length of the shadow of a mast 42·8 m tall

(b) the height of a tower whose shadow is 164·5 m long

4 Rates

4.1 A standard radio battery costs 58p and lasts for 210 hours. A super battery costs £1·45 and lasts for 650 hours. Which battery is better value for money? Explain how you decide.

4.2 In May 1985, £1 was worth 1·22 US dollars. It was also worth 310 Japanese yen. Use these figures to calculate the exchange rate between the dollar and the yen
(a) in yen per dollar   (b) in dollars per yen

4.3 The 08:45 train from London Euston arrives at Glasgow at 14:13. The 09:00 train from London Kings Cross arrives at Edinburgh at 14:10. The distance from Euston to Glasgow is 401·5 miles, and from Kings Cross to Edinburgh is 393 miles.

Calculate the average speed of each train.

4.4 This is the (time, temperature) graph for a cooling oven.

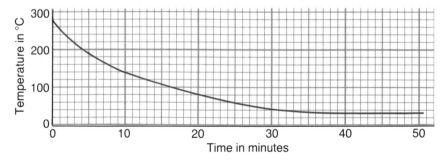

Calculate the average rate of fall of the temperature in deg./min between   (a) 0 min and 20 min   (b) 20 min and 50 min

4.5 This is the (time, distance) graph of a non-stop train travelling from Brighton to Victoria.

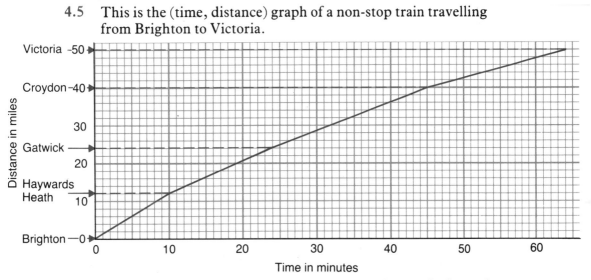

Time in minutes

(a) Calculate the average speed, in m.p.h., of the train for each part of the journey (between each station and the next).

(b) Calculate the average speed for the whole journey.

4.6 A car travelling at 50 m.p.h. does 25·3 miles on a gallon of petrol. How many minutes does it take to use up 1 gallon of petrol?

5 Algebraic expressions

5.1 Simplify these expressions where possible.
(a) $3p - 5q + 4p + q$ (b) $3a - 3 + 2a + 1$ (c) $pq - 3p + 2q$
(d) $2a - 3b + 5a + 7b$ (e) $5x - 4y - y - x$ (f) $r - 2s + 5r$
(g) $2a^2 - 3a + b^2 - 4a + b^2$ (h) $2pq - 3p - 5q + 4p - 3pq + p^2$
(i) $5x^2 - 2y^2 + 6xy + x^2 - 3y^2$ (j) $2s^2 - 3t - 4s + 5st - 7t^2$
(k) $4m - 2n + 5mn - n - 9m$ (l) $a - 2 + 4b - 3 - 5a + b$
(m) $2x^2 - 4xy - 3y^2 + 5xy - y^2$ (n) $15p^2 - pq - 7q^2 - 8pq + q^2$
(o) $a^2 - ab + b^2 - b - a - 1$ (p) $5a^2 - 2ab + 3b^2 - a^2 + 10ab$

5.2 Remove the brackets from these expressions and simplify.
(a) $5p - (p + 3)$ (b) $10y - (y - 5)$ (c) $7g + (2 - 3g)$
(d) $10s + (2 - 5s)$ (e) $6 - (4p - 9)$ (f) $3u - (2u + v)$
(g) $4x - (3 - 2x) + (5x - 1)$ (h) $12a + (3a - 2) - (4a - 5)$
(i) $3p + (2p - 5) - (4p - 2)$ (j) $10y - (y - 5) - (12 - 3y)$

5.3 Multiply out and simplify these.
(a) $5a - 2(a + 3)$ (b) $10x - 3(x - 5)$ (c) $7y - 4(2 - 3y)$
(d) $7x - 2(x - 3) + 5(x - 1)$ (e) $3p - 2(5 - 3p) - 4(6 - p)$
(f) $3a + 4(2a + 1) - 2(a - 3)$ (g) $5s + 3(2s - 4) - 5(s - 1)$
(h) $5x + 3(2x - 7y) + 2(x - 3y)$ (i) $4b - 2(3a - 2b) - 4(3b - a)$

5.4 Multiply out these expressions.
(a) $(x-3)(y-1)$ (b) $(a-2)(a+5)$ (c) $(2a-1)(a+5)$
(d) $(2p+3)(3p-4)$ (e) $(5x-3)(5x+3)$ (f) $(6x-1)^2$

5.5 Factorise these expressions.
(a) $6p-15q$ (b) $6pq-15q^2$ (c) $4+8a^2$ (d) $2ab-7b^2$
(e) $2ab+10b^2$ (f) $2ab-5bc$ (g) $10ab-5bc$ (h) $6ab+8a^2$

M Miscellaneous

M1 The Earth moves round the sun in an approximately circular orbit, the radius being about $9\cdot3 \times 10^7$ miles. One complete revolution takes $365\frac{1}{4}$ days.

Calculate the average speed in m.p.h. of the Earth in its orbit, to 2 s.f. Set out your working clearly.

M2 The area of a rectangle is 30 sq cm and the length of the rectangle is 2 cm more than its width. If w cm is the width, then $w(w+2)=30$.

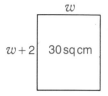

(a) Explain why w must be somewhere between 4 and 5.

(b) Use a decimal search to find the value of w, correct to 1 d.p.

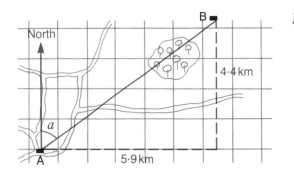

M3 A and B are two farmhouses. B is situated 5·9 km east and 4·4 km north of A.

(a) Use Pythagoras' rule to calculate the distance between A and B.

(b) Calculate the bearing of B from A. (It is the angle marked a in the diagram.)

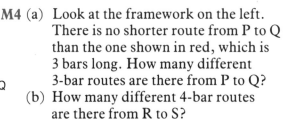

M4 (a) Look at the framework on the left. There is no shorter route from P to Q than the one shown in red, which is 3 bars long. How many different 3-bar routes are there from P to Q?

(b) How many different 4-bar routes are there from R to S?

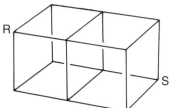

6 Trigonometry (2)

A The sine of an angle

The picture on the right shows an escalator. The sloping section is 12 metres long. It slopes at an angle of 35° to the horizontal.

The problem is to find how high the top of the escalator is above the bottom.

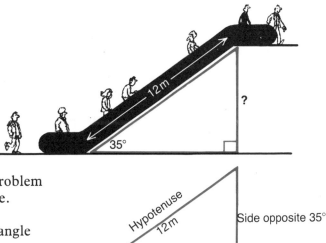

This may remind you of the type of problem where you use the tangent of the angle. But the tangent is used when you are dealing with the side **adjacent** to the angle and the side **opposite** the angle.

What we are given here is the **hypotenuse**.

In a right-angled triangle with an angle θ in it,	To calculate the side opposite θ, you

In a right-angled triangle with an angle θ in it,

the ratio $\dfrac{\text{side opposite } \theta}{\text{hypotenuse}}$ is called the **sine** of θ,

written **sin θ** (but pronounced sine θ).

To calculate the side opposite θ, you multiply the hypotenuse by sin θ.

Here is a table of the sines of some angles, to 3 decimal places.

θ	0°	5°	10°	15°	20°	25°	30°	35°	40°	45°
sin θ	0	0·087	0·174	0·259	0·342	0·423	0·500	0·574	0·643	0·707

θ	50°	55°	60°	65°	70°	75°	80°	85°	90°
sin θ	0·766	0·819	0·866	0·906	0·940	0·966	0·985	0·996	1

In the case of the escalator at the top of this page, the hypotenuse is 12 m and the angle is 35°.

So 12 × sin 35° = side opposite 35°.
So 12 × 0·574 = side opposite 35°.
So side opposite 35° = 6·9 m (to 1 d.p.).
The height of the top above the bottom is 6·9 m.

You may find it helpful to copy this diagram and formula into your book.

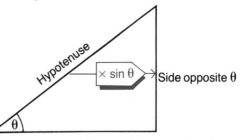

Hypotenuse × sin θ = side opposite θ

A1 Calculate the lengths marked with letters in these triangles. Use the table of sines on the previous page. Give answers to 1 d.p.

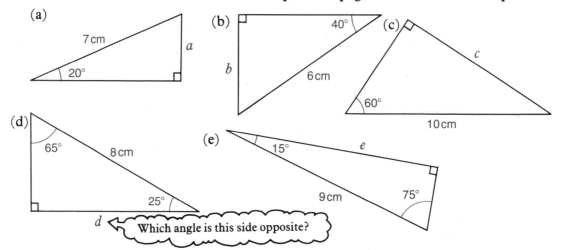

(a) 7 cm, 20°, a

(b) 40°, 6 cm, b

(c) c, 60°, 10 cm

(d) 65°, 8 cm, 25°, d — *Which angle is this side opposite?*

(e) 15°, e, 9 cm, 75°

Using a calculator

To find sin 40° on a calculator, enter 40 first and then press [sin].

To work out 12 × sin 40°, on most calculators you do this:

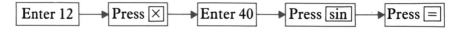

Enter 12 → Press × → Enter 40 → Press sin → Press =

A2 Calculate the lengths marked with letters, correct to 1 d.p.

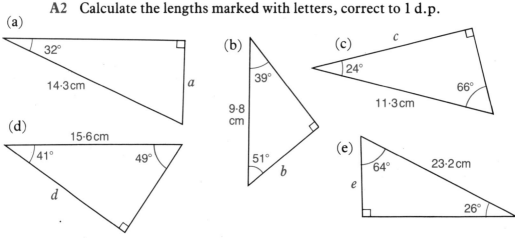

(a) 32°, 14·3 cm, a

(b) 39°, 9·8 cm, 51°, b

(c) c, 24°, 11·3 cm, 66°

(d) 15·6 cm, 41°, 49°, d

(e) 64°, 23·2 cm, e, 26°

This page has a mixture of problems on it.
Some of them require **sines** and some **tangents**.
As a reminder, here is the basic 'tangent' diagram.

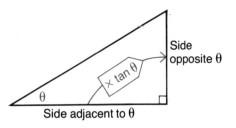

A3 Make a sketch of each triangle, and label its sides 'hyp' (hypotenuse),
'opp' (opposite the given angle) and 'adj' (adjacent to the given angle).
Decide whether to use sine or tangent to calculate the length asked for.

Give each answer correct to 1 decimal place.

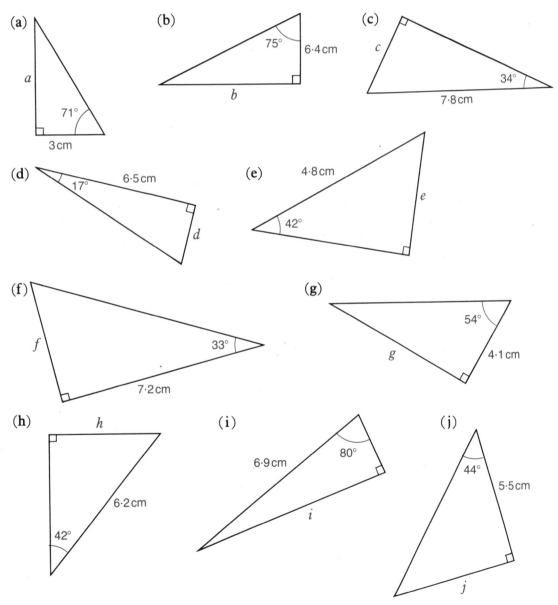

B The cosine of an angle

The cosine is another ratio which is useful for calculating
sides of right-angled triangles.

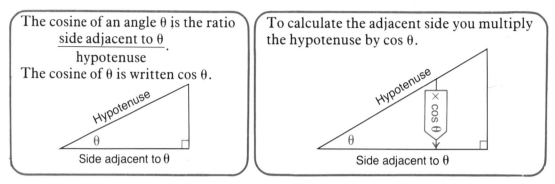

The cosine of an angle θ is the ratio
$$\frac{\text{side adjacent to } \theta}{\text{hypotenuse}}.$$
The cosine of θ is written cos θ.

To calculate the adjacent side you multiply
the hypotenuse by cos θ.

B1 Calculate the lengths marked with letters, to 1 d.p.

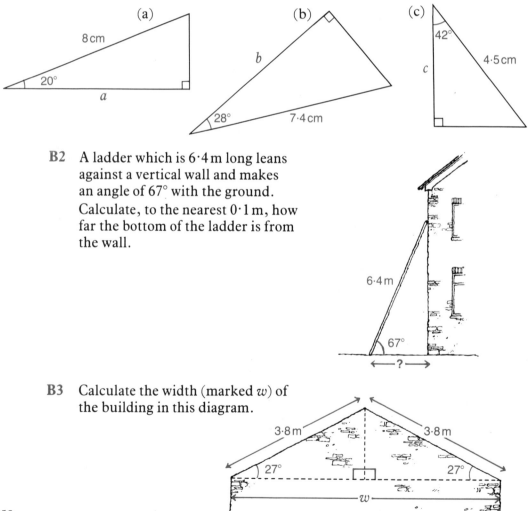

B2 A ladder which is 6·4 m long leans
against a vertical wall and makes
an angle of 67° with the ground.
Calculate, to the nearest 0·1 m, how
far the bottom of the ladder is from
the wall.

B3 Calculate the width (marked w) of
the building in this diagram.

c Calculating sides

Here is a good method to follow when you have to calculate one of the sides
of a right-angled triangle, given an angle.

1 Label the sides:
hyp (hypotenuse)
opp (opposite the given angle)
adj (adjacent to the given angle)

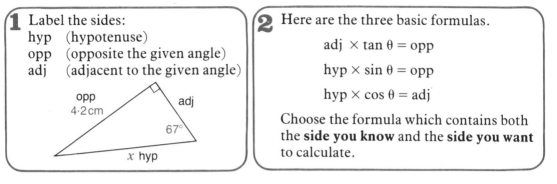

2 Here are the three basic formulas.

$$\text{adj} \times \tan \theta = \text{opp}$$

$$\text{hyp} \times \sin \theta = \text{opp}$$

$$\text{hyp} \times \cos \theta = \text{adj}$$

Choose the formula which contains both
the **side you know** and the **side you want**
to calculate.

C1 Calculate the lengths marked with letters, to 1 d.p.

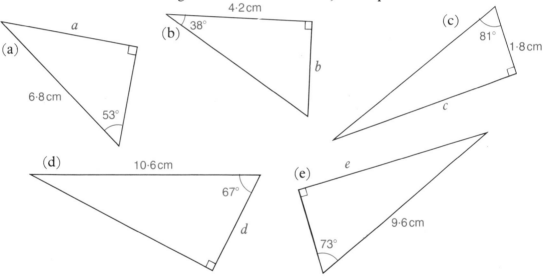

C2 Calculate the heights of the points A, B, C above the ground,
each to the nearest 0·1 m.

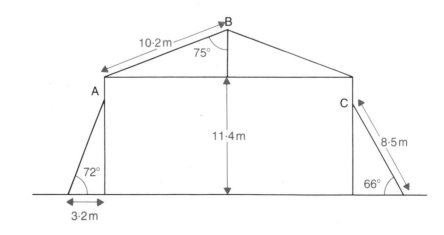

59

Sometimes when you put the values you know into the formula you end up with an equation to solve.

Worked example

Calculate the length marked p in this triangle.

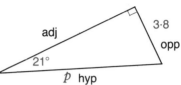

Here we know 'opp' and have to calculate 'hyp', so the formula to use is
$$\text{hyp} \times \sin \theta = \text{opp}.$$

So $\quad p \times \sin 21° = 3.8.$

So $\qquad\qquad p = \dfrac{3.8}{\sin 21°} = 10.6\,\text{cm (to 1 d.p.).}$

C3 Calculate the lettered sides of these triangles, to the nearest $0.1\,\text{cm}$.

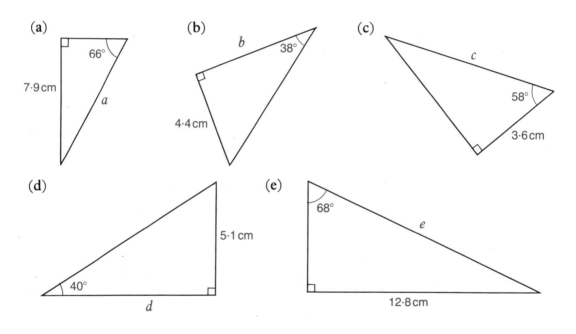

(a)

$66°$

$7.9\,\text{cm}$

a

(b)

b $38°$

$4.4\,\text{cm}$

(c)

c

$58°$

$3.6\,\text{cm}$

(d)

$5.1\,\text{cm}$

$40°$

d

(e)

$68°$

e

$12.8\,\text{cm}$

C4 This diagram shows the routes of two ferry boats across a river 38 metres wide.

(a) Calculate the length of the longer route, to the nearest metre.

(b) Calculate, to the nearest metre, the distance between the two points where the boats reach the opposite bank of the river.

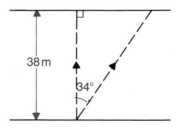

$38\,\text{m}$

$34°$

D Calculating angles

You can calculate an angle in a right-angled triangle
when you know the lengths of two of the sides.

Worked example

Calculate the angle θ in this triangle.

Here we know 'hyp' and 'adj', so the formula to use is
$$\text{hyp} \times \cos \theta = \text{adj}.$$

So $10{\cdot}6 \times \cos \theta = 4{\cdot}8.$

So $\cos \theta = \dfrac{4{\cdot}8}{10{\cdot}6} = 0{\cdot}45283 \ldots$

We now need to find the angle whose cosine is $0{\cdot}45283 \ldots$
It is the **inverse cosine** of $0{\cdot}45283 \ldots$
On most calculators you find it by entering $0{\cdot}45283 \ldots$ and pressing $\boxed{\text{inv}}$ $\boxed{\text{cos}}$.
The result (to the nearest degree) is 63°.

D1 Calculate, to the nearest degree, the angles marked with
letters in these triangles.

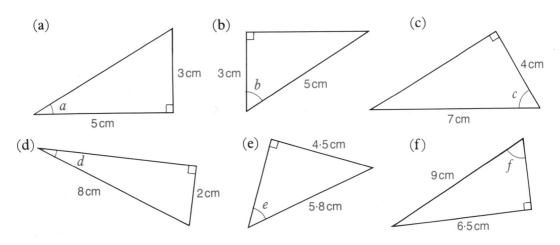

(a) 3cm, 5cm, a

(b) 3cm, 5cm, b

(c) 4cm, 7cm, c

(d) d, 8cm, 2cm

(e) 4·5cm, 5·8cm, e

(f) 9cm, 6·5cm, f

D2 A plank 5·3 metres long leans against the side wall of
a house. The foot of the plank is 2·1 metres from the wall.

Draw a sketch and calculate the angle which the plank
makes with the ground, to the nearest degree.

D3 A tree 2·50 metres tall casts a
shadow 4·36 metres long.

Calculate the angle of elevation of the
sun to the nearest degree. (The angle
is marked a in the diagram.)

E Mixed problems

The first step in answering each of these questions is to find
a suitable right-angled triangle in the diagram. You then
sketch the triangle, mark on it the measurements you know,
and use a letter for the side or angle you want to find.

Mark the sides of the triangle 'hyp', 'opp' and 'adj', and use
one of the basic formulas to calculate the unknown side or
angle.

In the first few questions the right-angled triangle has been
picked out for you in red.

E1 Calculate the angle which the line AB
makes with the horizontal, to the
nearest degree.

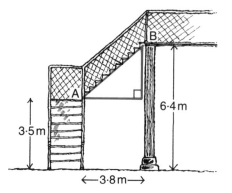

E2 (a) Calculate the height of the points P and Q
above the water level, to the nearest 0·1 metre.
(b) Calculate the distance between P and Q.

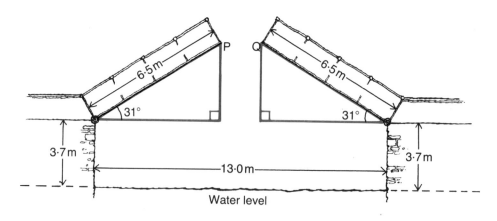

E3 Do question E2 again, but this time with each part
of the bridge making an angle of 48° with the horizontal.

E4 If the points P and Q in the diagram for question E2
are each 9·5 metres above the water level, what angle
does each part of the bridge make with the horizontal?

E5 The minute hand of the clock on the Royal Liver Building in Liverpool is 4·3 m long.

The centre of the clock face is 67 m above the ground.

(a) How high above the ground is the tip of the minute hand at 9:10 p.m.?

(b) How high is it above the ground at 10:25 a.m.?

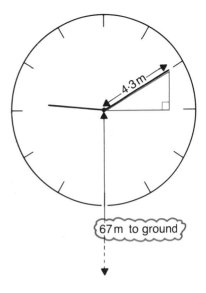

67 m to ground

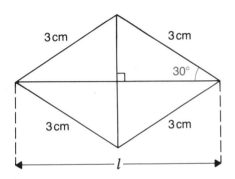

E6 Calculate the length marked *l* in this diagram.

Isosceles triangles

An **isosceles** triangle is one with two equal sides.

An isosceles triangle can be split into two identical right-angled triangles. This fact is often useful in calculations.

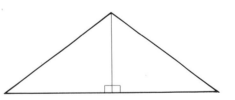

E7 ABC is an isosceles triangle. The angle ABC is 46°.

AB and BC are both 10 cm.

(a) What is the size of the angle marked θ?

(b) Calculate the length marked *a*, to the nearest 0·1 cm.

(c) Write down the length of AC.

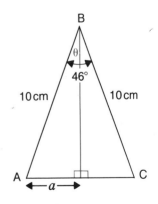

E8 Do question E7 again, but with AB and BC each 12 cm long, and the angle ABC 112°.

E9   Each angle of a regular pentagon is 108°.

If a regular pentagon has sides which are each 8 cm long, calculate the length of one of its diagonals, to the nearest 0·1 cm.

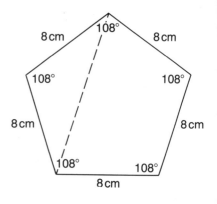

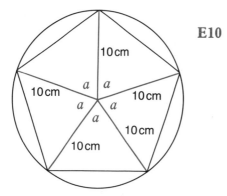

E10   A regular pentagon is drawn inside a circle of radius 10 cm.

(a)   What is the size of each of the angles marked a?

(b)   Calculate the length of one side of the pentagon, to the nearest 0·1 cm.

E11   PQR is an isosceles triangle.
PQ = QR = 6 cm.
PR = 4 cm.

Calculate the angle PQR, marked x, to the nearest degree.

(Split the triangle PQR into two right-angled triangles first.)

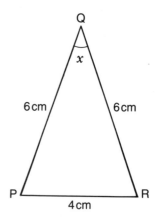

E12   Do question E11 again, but with PQ = QR = 5·6 cm, and PR = 3·7 cm.

E13   The sides of a rectangle are 10 cm and 7 cm long. Calculate the sizes of the angles between the diagonals of the rectangle.

E14   The diagonals of a rhombus are 14 cm and 8 cm long. Calculate each of the angles of the rhombus.

7 Investigations (1)

A Courses for horses

You need worksheet Y2–1.

This is a plan of a farm, with fields and hedges.

Each gap shows the position of a gate.

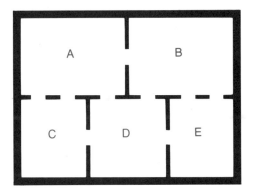

A1 A pony club wants to make a jumping course. The course can start in any one of the five fields, but it must go over every gate once and once only. It can finish in any of the fields.

Use diagram 1 on the worksheet to show a possible route for the course (if you can find one). Then answer these questions.

(a) In which field does your course start, and where does it finish? Could you have started and finished elsewhere?

(b) Can you find a course which starts in field A? If so, where does it finish?

A2 For each other diagram on the worksheet, try to find a route for a jumping course which goes over every gate once and once only.

For each diagram write down possible starting and finishing fields. If you think there is no possible route, write 'impossible'.

A3 Look at your diagrams carefully. Can you see what it is which makes it possible or impossible to find a route? If you have an idea what the rule might be, get *worksheet Y2–2* and try out your rule on diagrams 9 to 12. Use your rule to predict whether it will be possible or impossible to find a route, then see if your prediction is correct.

If you haven't any idea what the rule might be, ask your teacher to give you a hint.

If you think you have a rule which works for all the diagrams so far, try it out on some diagrams of your own. (Or better still, ask someone else to draw some diagrams for you.)

B Inspecting roads (1)

You need worksheet Y2–2.

B1 This map shows the roads on an island. A surveyor has to walk along every road to inspect them. She wonders if it is possible to do this without having to go along any road more than once.

Can she do it? If so, where should she start and finish? Use diagram 1 on the worksheet.

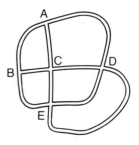

B2 On which other maps on the worksheet is it possible for the surveyor to walk along every road once and once only? Find possible starting and finishing places, or write 'impossible'.

Can you find a rule which allows you to say whether it will be possible or impossible to find a route for the surveyor? Try out your rule on the maps below.

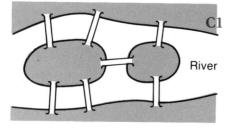
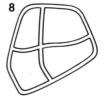
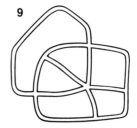

C The Koenigsberg Bridges problem

C1 The town of Koenigsberg (now called Kaliningrad) used to have seven bridges, as shown in this map. People wondered if it was possible to go for a walk crossing every bridge once and once only.

Is it possible? If not, why not?

D Inspecting roads (2)

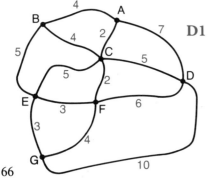

D1 A surveyor has to inspect every road in the network shown here. Distances are in miles.

(a) Can the surveyor make a tour of inspection walking along every road once and once only?

(b) If not, what is the shortest distance she needs to walk to be able to inspect every road? Where should she start and finish?

8 Distributions

A Distributions

A teacher is in charge of a class of 20 children. One morning he made a note of the time each child arrived at school. The arrival times are shown by markers on this scale.

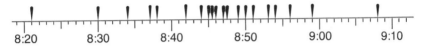

The children's arrival times are spread out, or **distributed**, between 8:21 and 9:08. But they are not distributed evenly. There are a lot of children in the middle and very few at each end.

We can divide the scale into intervals, and draw a chart to show the number of children arriving in each interval.
(A child who arrives at the 'boundary' between one interval and the next is counted as arriving in the interval to the right. So, for example, the child who arrived at 8:30 goes into the interval 8:30 to 8:40.)

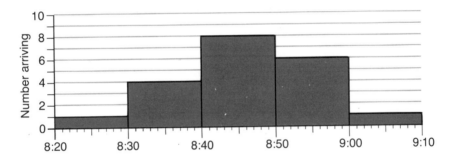

If you use different intervals, you get a different chart, but the general shape is the same (unless the intervals are very big or very small).

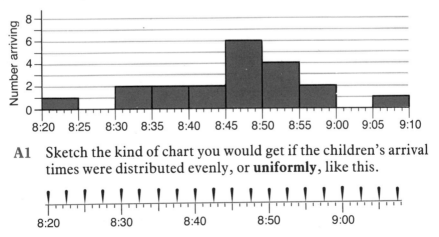

A1 Sketch the kind of chart you would get if the children's arrival times were distributed evenly, or **uniformly**, like this.

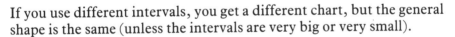

67

Several schools in and around a city were thinking of changing the time at which the school day ends. Some of the teachers were concerned about the time some of their pupils would be arriving home. So they decided to find out how long it took children to get from school to home (their 'journey times').

Here are the results for one of the primary schools.
The 'journey time' scale is divided into intervals. The chart shows the number of children whose journey times are in each interval.
These numbers are called **frequencies**. This chart, and those on the previous page, are called **frequency charts**.

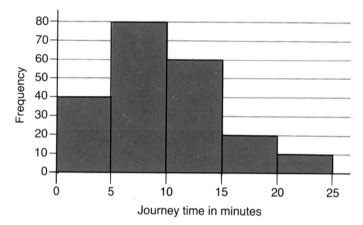

A2 (a) How many children have journey times of between 5 and 10 minutes?
(b) How many take 15 minutes or more to get home?
(c) How many children are there in the school?

When you look at the chart you may think that the longest journey time is 25 minutes. But the chart does not say this. It tells us that there are 10 children with journey times between 20 and 25 minutes, but it does not tell us what their actual journey times are. It may be that every one of these 10 children has a journey time of 21 minutes. We do not know. All we can say is that the longest journey time is somewhere between 20 and 25 minutes.

A3 What can you say about the shortest journey time?

The interval from 5 to 10 minutes has more children in it than any of the other intervals. The interval from 5 to 10 minutes is called the **modal** interval. ('Modal' comes from 'mode', and means 'most popular'.)

A4 What percentage of the children have journey times which are in the modal interval? (Give the answer to the nearest 5%.)

A5 If school were to end at 3:45 p.m., what percentage of the children would get home at 4 p.m. or later?

The frequency chart on the opposite page shows how the children's journey times are spread out or **distributed**.
We say the chart shows the **frequency distribution** of the journey times.

The chart below shows the frequency distribution of journey times in another school. This school is further away from the city, in a village.

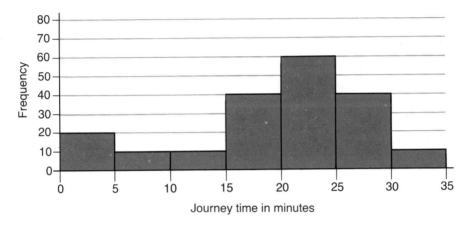

A6 What can you say about the longest journey time of a pupil in the village school?

A7 What is the modal interval of journey times?

A8 (a) How many pupils are there at the village school?
(b) How many of them take 20 minutes or more to get home?

A9 If school were to end at 3:45 p.m., what percentage of the pupils would get home at 4 p.m. or later?

A10 Draw a rough sketch of the kind of frequency chart of journey times you would expect to get for each of these schools.

(a) A school in a housing estate where all the pupils live very close to the school

(b) A school which serves two towns some distance apart. The school is situated in one of the towns. About half of the pupils come from this town and about half from the other one

(c) A school where most of the pupils live nearby, but a few live quite a long way away

(d) A school where all the pupils come long distances from home

A11 Think about your own school, and draw a rough sketch of a frequency chart showing the distribution of journey times from school to home.

B Mean values

The scale below shows the weights of
the 8 forwards in a rugby team.

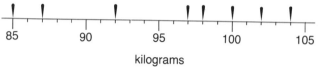

kilograms

The weights are distributed between 85 and 104 kilograms.

It is often useful to have a single value which gives some
idea of the weights (or heights, etc.) in a group.
The most common way of doing this is to calculate the
mean of the measurements in the group.

The **mean weight** of the 8 forwards is found by adding the
weights together and dividing by 8.

$$\text{Mean weight} = \frac{85 + 87 + 92 + 97 + 98 + 100 + 102 + 104}{8} = 95 \cdot 6 \, \text{kg}$$
(to 1 d.p.)

Here is the scale again, with the mean marked on it.
Notice that the mean is somewhere 'in the middle' of the weights.
Some of the weights are less than the mean and some are greater.

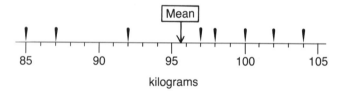

Mean

kilograms

B1 The weights of the 8 forwards in the opposing team are
(in kilograms)

84, 89, 94, 97, 101, 101, 104, 106

Calculate the mean weight of these forwards.

B2 The mean weight of the 11 players in a
women's hockey team is 69 kg.
(a) What is the total weight of the team?
(b) One of the players, who weighs 75 kg, is
replaced by a player weighing 80·5 kg.
By how much does the mean weight of
the team go up?

B3 The midday temperature on Monday, Tuesday and Wednesday
was 16 °C. On Thursday, Friday, Saturday and Sunday it was
19 °C. Calculate the mean midday temperature that week.

70

A firm making boxes of matches decided to check the contents of the boxes. They took 50 boxes and counted the matches in each box. Here are the results.

Number of matches in box	Number of boxes	Number of matches
45	10	450
46	23	1058
47	17	799
Totals	50	2307

This column shows the number of matches in each group of boxes.

For example, there were 10 boxes with 45 matches in each box, making $45 \times 10 = 450$ matches.

Altogether, 50 boxes contained 2307 matches.

So the mean number of matches per box was $\dfrac{2307}{50} = 46 \cdot 14$.

Notice that the mean here is not a whole number, even though the number of matches in any actual box must be a whole number.

B4   This table shows the results of counting the number of seeds in 40 packets of seeds.

(a) Copy the table and complete it.

(b) Calculate the mean number of seeds per packet.

Number of seeds in packet	Number of packets	Number of seeds
20	25	
21	12	
22	3	
Totals		

This frequency chart shows the weights of all the 12-year-old boys in a school.

We cannot calculate accurately the mean weight of the boys, because we do not know the weight of each boy and so cannot find the total weight.

All we know is that there were 10 boys weighing from 20 to 25 kg, and so on.

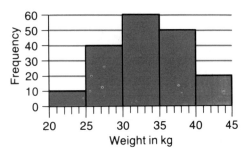

There is a way of getting a rough value, or **estimate**, of the total weight. We suppose that all the 10 boys in the 20 to 25 kg group have a weight which is halfway between 20 and 25 kg, that is, 22·5 kg. 22·5 kg is called the **mid-interval value** of the interval 20 to 25 kg. We do a similar thing for each of the other intervals.

Weight in kg	Mid-interval value	Number of boys	Weight of group, in kg
20–25	22·5	10	225
25–30			
30–35			
35–40			
40–45			
Totals			

B5   (a) Copy and complete the table on the left, using the chart above.

(b) Calculate an estimate of the mean weight of the boys, to the nearest kilogram.

71

Here again is the frequency chart for the boys' weights, with the estimated mean marked on it.

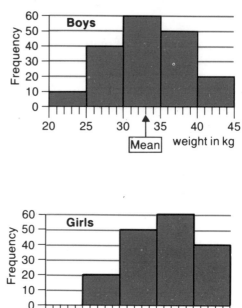

B6 This is the frequency chart of the girls' weights in the same school.

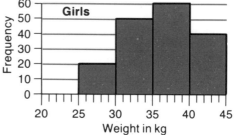

(a) Make a table, like the one in question B5, for the girls' weights.

(b) Calculate an estimate of the mean weight of the girls.

(c) Are the girls heavier or lighter on the whole than the boys?

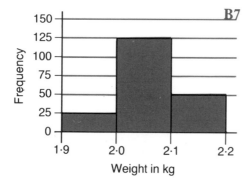

B7 This chart shows the distribution of the weights of 200 bags of sugar taken from a factory.

(a) What is the mid-interval value of the interval 1·9 to 2·0 kg?

(b) Use mid-interval values to calculate an estimate of the total weight of the bags.

(c) Calculate an estimate of the mean weight of the bags.

B8 This chart shows how the lengths of 125 phone calls were distributed.

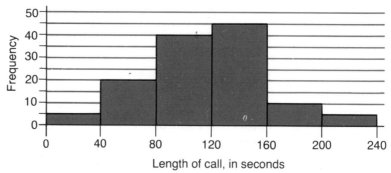

(a) Estimate the mean length of a call.

(b) What percentage of calls lasted 2 minutes or longer?

c Limitations of the mean

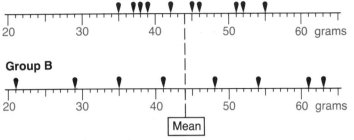

These scales show the weights of the tomatoes obtained from two different plants.

The mean weight is the same for each group of tomatoes.

The mean weight of each group is the same, but in another way the two groups are different from each other. The second group is much more widely spread out than the first. The mean tells you nothing about this.

When you are describing a group of numbers (weights, heights, etc.) it is a good idea to give the lowest and highest values as well as the mean value. The size of the difference between the lowest and highest values is called the **range**, and this tells you how wide the spread of the numbers is.

So the weights of the tomatoes in group A can be described like this:

   Mean weight 44 g   Lightest 35 g   Heaviest 55 g   Range 20 g

   C1   Describe the tomatoes in group B in the same way.

Sometimes the mean value of a group of numbers can give a very misleading idea of the group.

A firm employing 10 people said that the mean wage of its employees was £93 per week. This gives the impression that £93 is a kind of 'middle' figure, with some workers getting a bit more and some a bit less. But how much more, and how much less? The mean tells us nothing about this.

Here are the actual wages of the 10 employees.

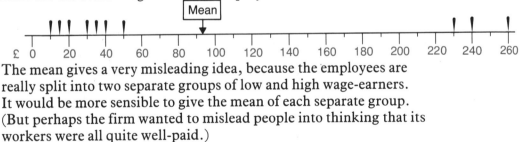

The mean gives a very misleading idea, because the employees are really split into two separate groups of low and high wage-earners. It would be more sensible to give the mean of each separate group. (But perhaps the firm wanted to mislead people into thinking that its workers were all quite well-paid.)

   C2   Here are the ages of the people on a coach outing.

   9, 8, 9, 9, 10, 8, 10, 10, 9, 42, 8, 9, 9, 8, 8, 53, 8, 9, 9, 10, 10, 9

   (a) Does it make sense to calculate the mean age of the whole group? If not, why not?
   (b) Calculate the mean age of the children in the group.

73

D Motorcycle accidents

A survey of motorcycle accidents was carried out recently. The investigators were interested in the ages of the motorcyclists and the speeds at which the accidents occurred.

D1 This chart shows the distribution of the ages of 395 motorcyclists involved in accidents.

The numbers on the columns are the frequencies.

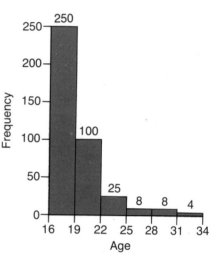

(a) What percentage of those involved in accidents were
   (i) under the age of 25 (ii) over 25
(b) Use the mid-interval method to calculate an estimate of the mean age of the injured motorcyclists.
(c) Can you suggest a reason why the age group which has the largest number of accidents is the 16 to 19 age group?

D2 An investigation of the speeds at which accidents occurred yielded this distribution.

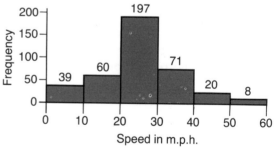

(a) Can you suggest a reason why motorcycle accidents most frequently occurred at speeds between 20 and 30 m.p.h.?
(b) Calculate an estimate of the mean value of the speeds at which the accidents occurred.

It is very easy to misunderstand the chart in question D2.
The chart **seems** to be saying that it is very safe to ride at a high speed,
because very few accidents occur at high speeds. But the reason why
very few accidents occur at high speeds is because very few motorcyclists ride
at high speed. (Or if they do, they only do it for part of the time.)

Imagine 120 motorcyclists.
100 of them ride at low speeds and 20 of them at high speeds.
Suppose 15 of the 'low' group and 10 of the 'high' group have accidents.

In the 'low' group, 15 out of 100,
or 15%, have accidents.

In the 'high' group, 10 out of 20,
or 50%, have accidents.

So the 'high' group have a worse accident record, even though
their actual number of accidents was smaller.

D3 In a group of 450 reported motorcycle accidents, the injuries to
the motorcyclists were classified into three kinds:
Minor casualties   Moderate casualties   Severe or fatal casualties

The distribution of the speeds of the motorcyclists at the time of the
accidents is shown below for each of the three kinds of injury.

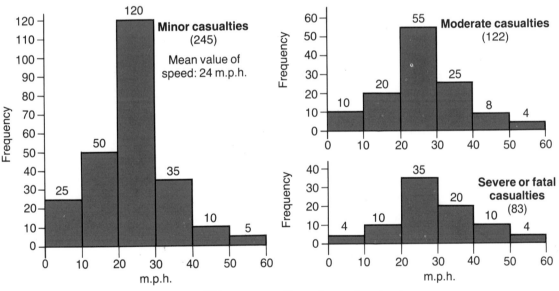

(a) There were 450 motorcyclists altogether in the group.
What percentage of them were   (i) minor casualties   (ii) moderate
casualties   (iii) severe or fatal casualties
(b) There were 245 minor casualties. In what percentage of them
was the motorcyclist travelling at over 30 m.p.h.?
(c) Calculate the percentage of motorcyclists travelling at over 30 m.p.h.
for each of the other kinds of injury.
(d) The mean value of the speeds of the minor casualties was 24 m.p.h.
Calculate estimates of the mean value of the speeds of
(i) the moderate casualties   (ii) the severe or fatal casualties

75

E Collecting data

This section consists of experiments which a whole class can do together. The first one is described in detail.

E1 Estimating a time interval of 1 minute

Each person works with a partner. You will need a watch which shows seconds. Call yourselves A and B.

To start with, A has the watch and says 'Start'.
B says 'Stop' when he or she thinks 1 minute has passed.
A notes down the number of seconds in B's 'minute'.
Then A and B change places.

(a) Make a tally table of the results of the whole class.

(b) Draw a frequency chart.

(c) Find the mean length of the estimated 'minutes'.

(d) Each person can mark the mean and his or her own estimate on the scale of the frequency chart.

Time in sec		Frequency
40–45	ⵑⵑⵑ lll	8
45–50	ⵑⵑⵑ ⵑⵑⵑ ll	12
:	:	:

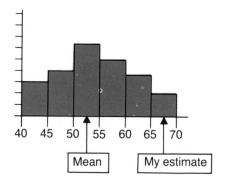

40   45   50   55   60   65   70

Mean   My estimate

E2 Estimating the size of an angle

The teacher draws an angle on a sheet of paper and holds it up or passes it round. Each person estimates the size of the angle.

E3 Drawing an angle of 30° without any instruments except a straight edge

Each person measures the angle they have drawn, and the results are collected together.

E4 Estimating the number of spots on a sheet of paper

The teacher makes some large spots on a sheet of paper (or overhead projector transparency) and shows them briefly to the whole class. Each person estimates the number of spots.

E5 Estimating the length of a line

The teacher draws a line on the blackboard. Each person estimates its length in centimetres.

9 Re-arranging formulas (1)

A Equations from formulas

A car travels at a constant speed of s metres per second for t seconds.
If d metres is the distance it travels, then d is given by the formula

$$d = st.$$

A1 Calculate d when (a) $s = 3, t = 8$ (b) $s = 5 \cdot 8, t = 12 \cdot 5$

Sometimes we know the values of d and s, and we want to find t.
For example, suppose $d = 56$ and $s = 35$. We replace d and s in the formula
by their values, and we get an equation to solve.

$$56 = 35t$$

Divide both sides by 35. $\quad \dfrac{56}{35} = \dfrac{35t}{35}$

$$1 \cdot 6 = t$$

A2 Calculate t when $d = 81 \cdot 6$ and $s = 8 \cdot 5$. Write out the working as above.

A3 Calculate s when $d = 690 \cdot 3$ and $t = 11 \cdot 8$.

A4 p, q, r and s are connected by the formula $q = pr + s$.
(a) Write down the equation you get when $q = 17, p = 4$ and $r = 2$.
(b) Solve the equation to find the value of s.
(c) Write down the equation you get when $q = 38, p = 5$ and $s = 3$.
(d) Solve the equation to find the value of r.

A5 The formula $I = \dfrac{V}{R}$ is used by electricians.
(a) Write down the equation you get when $I = 20$ and $R = 4$.
(b) Solve the equation to find the value of V.
(c) Write down the equation you get when $I = 0 \cdot 8$ and $R = 12 \cdot 5$.
(d) Solve the equation to find the value of V.

A6 a, b, c and d are connected by the formula $d = a - bc$.
(a) Write down the equation you get when $d = 19, b = 4$ and $c = 3$.
(b) Solve the equation to find a.
(c) Write down the equation you get when $d = 17, a = 62$ and $b = 3$.
(d) Solve the equation to find c.

A7 t, u, v and w are connected by the formula $t = u + vw$.
Calculate the value of v when $t = 93, u = 66$ and $w = 9$.

B Re-arranging a formula

On the previous page we met the formula $d = st$ and used it to find t when d and s are known. If we have to do many calculations of this type, it is better to have a formula for calculating t directly. Then we do not have to solve an equation every time.

The formula $d = st$ tells you how to calculate d when you know s and t. We say it gives d **in terms of** s and t, and we call d the **subject** of the formula. We want a formula for t in terms of d and s, so we want to make t the subject.

We get the formula for t by thinking of $d = st$ as an equation in which d and s are known numbers, but t is unknown. We solve the equation in exactly the same way as we would with numbers in place of d and s.

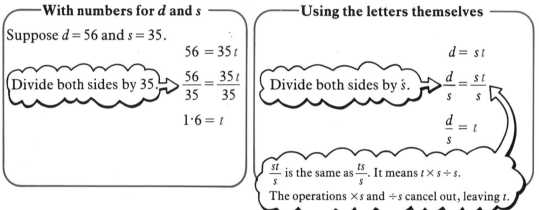

Going from $d = st$ to $\dfrac{d}{s} = t$ is called **re-arranging** the formula.

B1 (a) Re-arrange the formula $d = st$ to give s in terms of d and t. Write out the working as in the right-hand panel above.
    (b) Use your new formula to find s when $d = 6 \cdot 3$ and $t = 18$.

B2 Re-arrange the formula $f = nw$ to give w in terms of f and n.

B3 Re-arrange the formula $q = p + a$ to give p in terms of q and a.

B4 Re-arrange the formula $c = \dfrac{m}{n}$ to give m in terms of c and n.

B5 Re-arrange the formula $d = r - s$ to give r in terms of d and s.

B6 Re-arrange each of these formulas to make the letter printed in red the subject of the formula.
    (a) $y = 3x$ (b) $y = kx$ (c) $y = kx$ (d) $g = m - a$
    (e) $g = m + a$ (f) $g = m + a$ (g) $s = \dfrac{t}{5}$ (h) $s = \dfrac{t}{k}$

B7 Re-arrange the formula $p = 3m + a$ to give m in terms of p and a.

C Further re-arrangements

If you have to re-arrange a formula, it may help if you replace the letters whose values are supposed to be known, by 'easy' numbers. Solve the equation you get, and then follow the same steps with the letters themselves.

Example

Re-arrange $v = u + at$ to give a in terms of v, u and t.

We suppose v, u and t are known, and we want to find a.

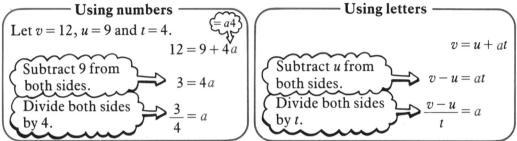

After some practice you should be able to work with the letters directly.

C1 Re-arrange the formula $y = ax + b$ to give x in terms of y, a and b.

C2 Re-arrange each of these formulas to make the letter printed in red the subject of the formula.

(a) $q = 4p + a$ (b) $q = kp + a$ (c) $q = kp + a$
(d) $q = kp + a$ (e) $m = af - t$ (f) $w = u + kv$
(g) $w = u + kv$ (h) $w = u + kv$ (i) $t = m - np$

Worked example

Re-arrange $c = \dfrac{a}{n} + b$ to give a in terms of c, n and b.

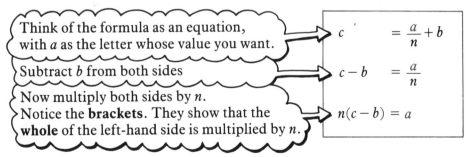

C3 Re-arrange the formula $k = \dfrac{s}{p} - a$ to give s in terms of k, a and p.

C4 Re-arrange the formula $d = a + \dfrac{c}{n}$ to give c in terms of d, a and n.

C5 Re-arrange each of these formulas to make x the subject.

(a) $q = \dfrac{x}{p} - r$ (b) $r = q + \dfrac{x}{p}$ (c) $p = \dfrac{x}{r} + q$

10 Points, lines and planes

A Impossible objects

The picture on the opposite page was drawn by the Dutch artist M. C. Escher.
It shows an impossible building. The seated boy at the bottom of the
picture is holding a very peculiar object, and there is a sketch of the
same object at his feet. Although we can draw this object we cannot
make a model of it. It is another impossible object.

In this picture the boy is balancing
an impossible object, often called a 'blivet'.

This looks rather like a blivet, but
this is not an impossible object.
It could be made.

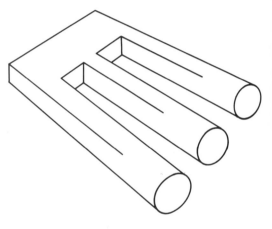

This, however, looks quite possible but is not.

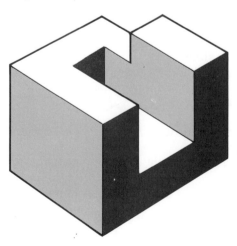

Often you can look at a picture and see quite easily that
it shows an impossible object. In other cases it is not so easy to decide.

Sometimes a drawing shows an 'object' made up of lines and flat surfaces.
But the lines and surfaces are arranged in an impossible way.
You can only tell that they are impossible if you know what arrangements
really are possible.

That is what we shall be studying in this chapter.

82

B One plane

In this picture of a cube... ...you can see parts of **3 planes.**

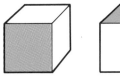

A plane is flat, and it is important to realise that it does not stop at the bit you can actually see. It extends as far as you like in all directions.

 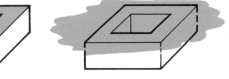

What you can see may have a gap in it, but the plane does not.

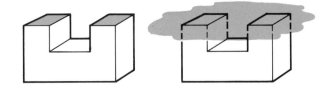

B1 Here are two models. The surfaces which are visible are lettered. In model (a), the surfaces *d* and *e* are parts of the same plane.

For each model, say which surfaces go together as parts of the same plane.

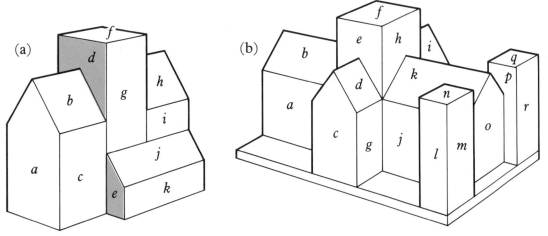

(a)

(b)

This picture seems to show a plane passing behind itself, which is impossible.

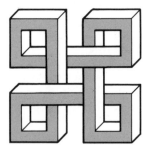

B2 Which of these pictures show impossible objects?

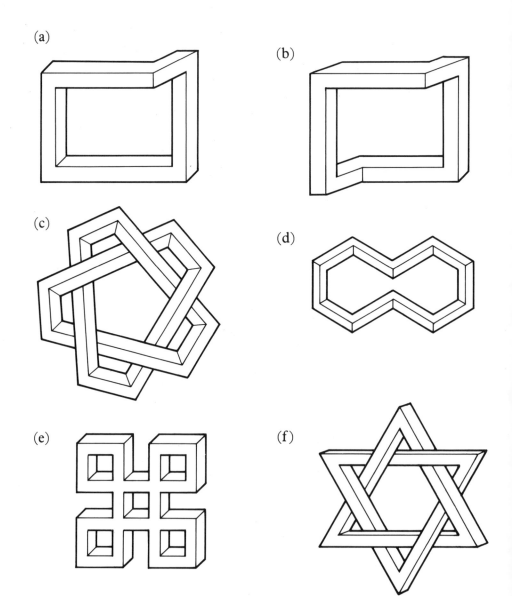

(a)

(b)

(c)

(d)

(e)

(f)

C Two planes

You need worksheet Y2–3.

When two planes meet, they make a straight **line** where they meet.

Each plane extends as far as you like.
The line where they meet stretches as far as you like in both directions.

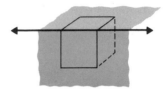

In your classroom, the walls are probably parts of planes.
So are the ceiling and the floor. Look for the lines where two planes meet.

Sometimes the parts of planes which we can see do not meet, but when we extend them we find the lines still exist.

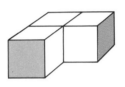

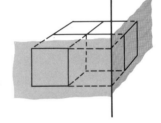

C1 The surface AFIH is part of one plane. The surface CDEG is part of another plane.

The line where the two planes meet is one of the lines in the picture. Which line is it?

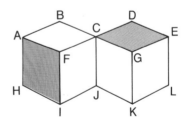

C2 Do two planes always meet?

C3 These diagrams are reproduced on worksheet Y2–3. In each case draw on the worksheet the line where the two shaded planes meet.

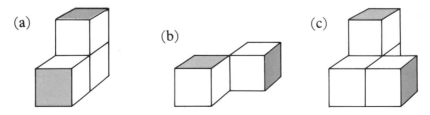

Parallel planes

Two planes do not always meet.
They may be **parallel** to each other.
In that case they never meet, but are
the same distance apart everywhere.

In your classroom the floor and ceiling are
probably parallel to each other.

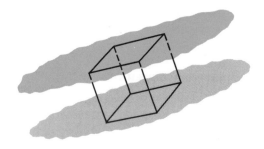

An impossible object

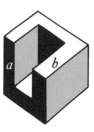

At first glance, it looks as though this object might be possible.
But what we know about two planes meeting in a line shows
that the object is not possible.

The two planes *a* (front) and *b* (top)
should meet in **one** line.

But according to the picture they meet
in two different lines! This is impossible.

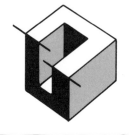

C4 Which of these pictures show impossible objects?

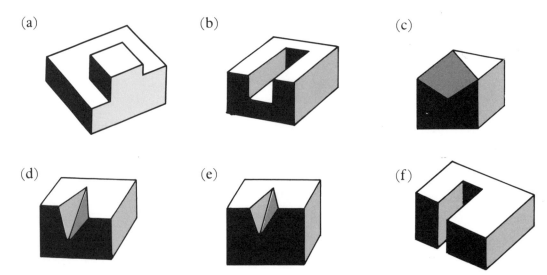

(a)

(b)

(c)

(d)

(e)

(f)

D   A plane and a line

If we have one plane and one line, three different things can happen.

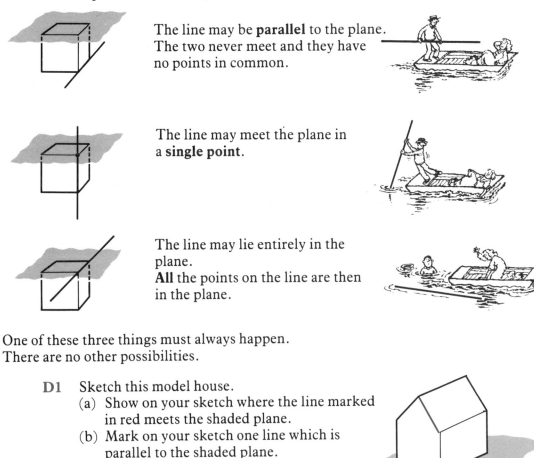

The line may be **parallel** to the plane. The two never meet and they have no points in common.

The line may meet the plane in a **single point**.

The line may lie entirely in the plane.
All the points on the line are then in the plane.

One of these three things must always happen.
There are no other possibilities.

D1   Sketch this model house.
   (a) Show on your sketch where the line marked in red meets the shaded plane.
   (b) Mark on your sketch one line which is parallel to the shaded plane.

D2   Does this picture show a possible object? If not, why not?

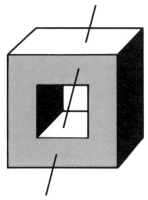

D3   What about these?

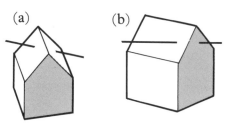

(a)   (b)

(c)

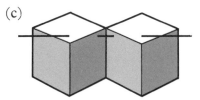

E Three planes

Next we look at what can happen if we have three planes, a, b and c.

One possibility is that they are all parallel,
rather like the layers of a sandwich.

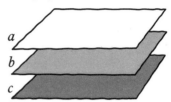

Otherwise two of the planes must meet, making a line.
Suppose a and b meet in a line. Then there are three things
which could happen.

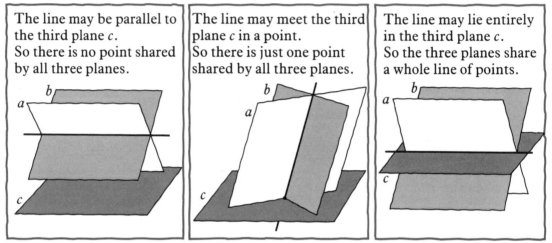

| The line may be parallel to the third plane c. So there is no point shared by all three planes. | The line may meet the third plane c in a point. So there is just one point shared by all three planes. | The line may lie entirely in the third plane c. So the three planes share a whole line of points. |

E1 Find an example in your classroom of three planes which meet in a single point.

E2 These diagrams are on worksheet Y2–3. On the worksheet mark the point where the three shaded planes meet.

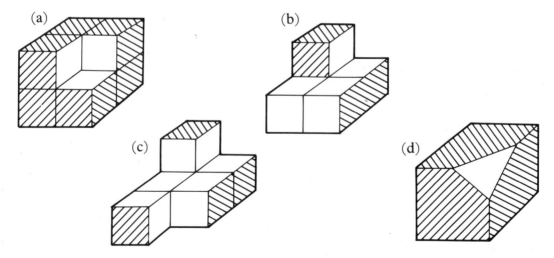

(a)

(b)

(c)

(d)

88

An impossible object

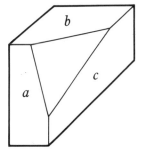

Planes a, b and c should meet at a point.

Line 1 contains all the points shared by planes a and b.

Line 2 contains all the points shared by planes b and c.

Line 3 contains all the points shared by planes c and a.

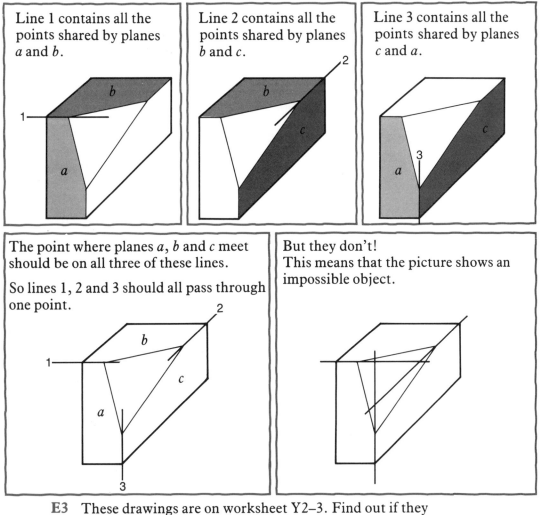

The point where planes a, b and c meet should be on all three of these lines.

So lines 1, 2 and 3 should all pass through one point.

But they don't!
This means that the picture shows an impossible object.

E3 These drawings are on worksheet Y2–3. Find out if they show impossible objects.

(a)

(b)

(c)

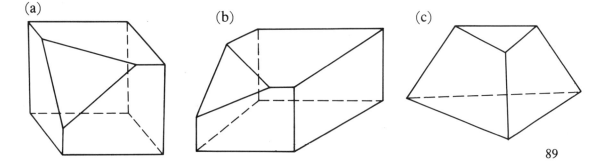

E4 These drawings are on worksheet Y2–3. Find out if they show impossible objects.

(a)

(b)

(c)

E5 This is a collection of miscellaneous 'objects'. Which of these drawings show impossible objects?

(a)

(b)

(c)

(d)

(e)

(f)

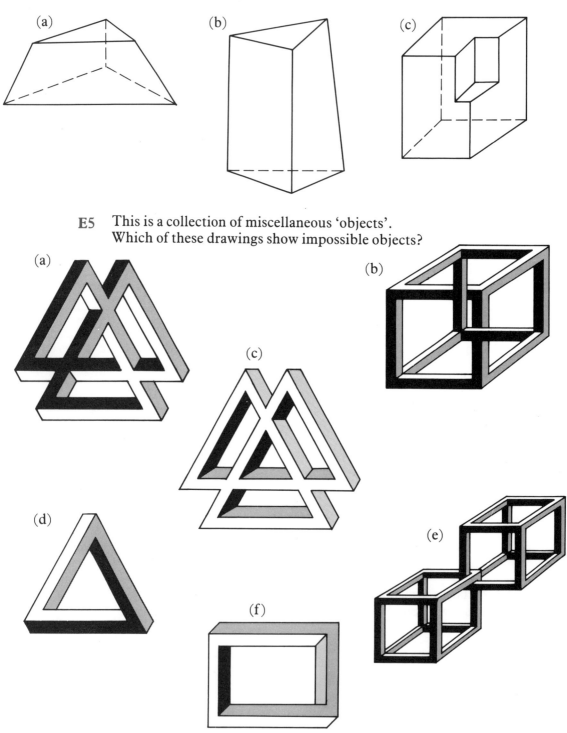

E6 Try to draw an impossible object of your own.

F Trick objects

The two photos on this page seem to show models of impossible objects!
The photos have not been re-touched or faked in any way.

Can you work out how they were taken?

The Penrose triangle

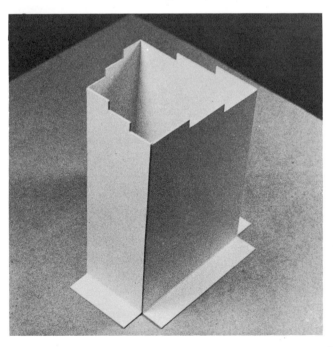

The Penrose staircase

These objects are entirely possible,
but when they are viewed from
a particular direction the eye is tricked.
We think we are seeing an
impossible object.

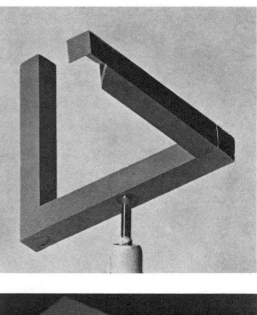

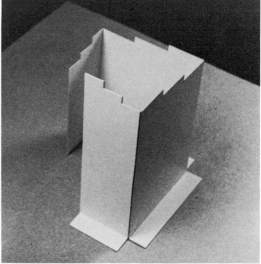

On the opposite page is a net for a 'Penrose staircase'.
Mark it out carefully on thin card.

Cut along the solid lines.

Fold along the dotted lines as shown in diagram ①.

On another piece of card, draw a square of side 60 mm ②.

Glue the four tabs a, b, c, d round the square, as in diagram ③.

To view the 'staircase', close one eye. Move your head
until corners A and B are exactly in line.

All dimensions are in millimetres.

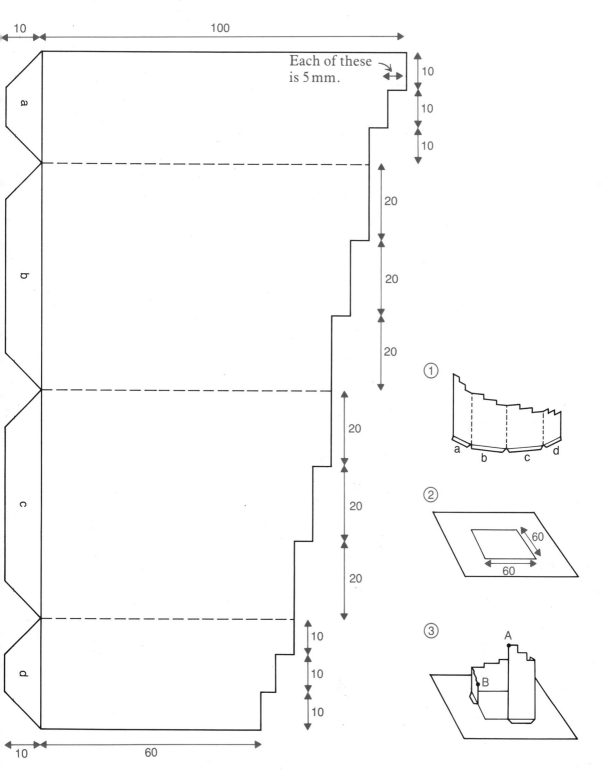

Each of these is 5 mm.

①
②
③

11 Re-arranging formulas (2)

A Further re-arrangements (1)

Look at this formula: $a = b - x$.

Suppose you want to re-arrange it to give x in terms of a and b.
You could start, as before, by replacing a and b by numbers.

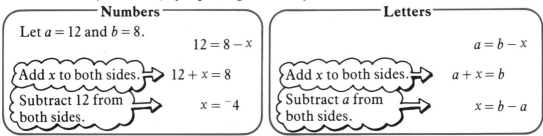

Numbers

Let $a = 12$ and $b = 8$.

$$12 = 8 - x$$

Add x to both sides. ⟹ $12 + x = 8$

Subtract 12 from both sides. ⟹ $x = {}^-4$

Letters

$$a = b - x$$

Add x to both sides. ⟹ $a + x = b$

Subtract a from both sides. ⟹ $x = b - a$

A similar method can be used to re-arrange the formula $p = q - kt$
to give t in terms of p, q and k.

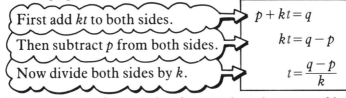

First add kt to both sides. ⟹ $p + kt = q$

Then subtract p from both sides. ⟹ $kt = q - p$

Now divide both sides by k. ⟹ $t = \dfrac{q - p}{k}$

A1   Re-arrange the formula $h = f - g$ to give g in terms of h and f.
(Start by adding g to both sides.)

A2   Re-arrange the formula $r = s - tx$ to give t in terms of r, s and x.
(Start by adding tx to both sides. Then subtract r from both sides.)

In questions A3 to A6, re-arrange each formula to give the letter printed in red.

A3   (a) $k = x - y$ (b) $b = a - ky$ (c) $b = a - ky$ (d) $y = ab - px$

A4 $d = c - \dfrac{m}{a}$. (Start by adding $\dfrac{m}{a}$ to both sides. Then subtract d from
both sides. Then multiply both sides by a. Don't forget the brackets!)

A5   (a) $s = a - \dfrac{b}{c}$ (b) $f = 3 - \dfrac{x}{n}$ (c) $k = b - \dfrac{z}{4}$ (d) $q = ap - \dfrac{r}{s}$

A6   Here is a mixture of the types you have met so far in this book.

(a) $t = au - b$ (b) $f = \dfrac{m}{u}$ (c) $r = p - qs$ (d) $z = uw$

(e) $y = mx + c$ (f) $d = f + pr$ (g) $k = \dfrac{s}{n} + m$ (h) $w = a - \dfrac{x}{s}$

B Further re-arrangements (2)

The formula $C = 2\pi r$ is used to calculate the circumference, C, of a circle when you know its radius, r.
If you want to re-arrange the formula to give r, there are two ways of doing it.

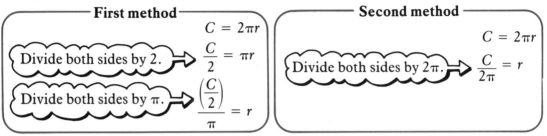

First method

$C = 2\pi r$

Divide both sides by 2. $\Rightarrow$ $\dfrac{C}{2} = \pi r$

Divide both sides by π. $\Rightarrow$ $\dfrac{\left(\dfrac{C}{2}\right)}{\pi} = r$

Second method

$C = 2\pi r$

Divide both sides by 2π. $\Rightarrow$ $\dfrac{C}{2\pi} = r$

Both methods are correct, but the second method leads to a simpler formula.
So the second method is the one usually used.

B1 Re-arrange the formula $v = pxy$ to give y in terms of v, p and x.
(Divide both sides by px.)

B2 Re-arrange the formula $d = fhs$ to make f the subject.

B3 Re-arrange the formula $z = mst$ to make s the subject.
(Divide both sides by mt.)

B4 Re-arrange each of these formulas to give the letter in red.
    (a) $t = prs$ (b) $m = fgkw$ (c) $s = 3rty$ (d) $k = a^2bc$

Worked example

Re-arrange the formula $s = \dfrac{3uv}{bn}$ to give u in terms of s, v, b and n.

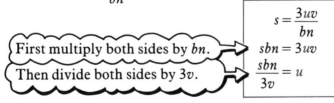

First multiply both sides by bn. $\Rightarrow$

Then divide both sides by $3v$. $\Rightarrow$

$s = \dfrac{3uv}{bn}$

$sbn = 3uv$

$\dfrac{sbn}{3v} = u$

B5 Re-arrange the formula $A = \dfrac{bh}{2}$ to give h in terms of A and b.

B6 Re-arrange each of these formulas to give the letter in red.
    (a) $I = \dfrac{PRT}{100}$ (b) $I = \dfrac{PRT}{100}$ (c) $I = \dfrac{PRT}{100}$ (d) $Y = \dfrac{Fl}{Ae}$

    (e) $Y = \dfrac{Fl}{Ae}$ (f) $k = \dfrac{abs}{tuv}$ (g) $f = \dfrac{lm}{pqr}$ (h) $V = \frac{1}{3}\pi r^2 h$

c Using a calculator

On the previous page, two different methods were used to re-arrange the formula $C = 2\pi r$.

One method led to $r = \dfrac{\left(\dfrac{C}{2}\right)}{\pi}$ and the other to $r = \dfrac{C}{2\pi}$.

Although the second one is simpler to write, the first is easier to use with a calculator.

Suppose you want to find r when $C = 7$.

If you use the first formula, your key sequence would be this.

If you use the second formula, you need brackets in the key sequence.

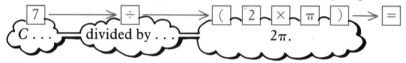

If you leave out the brackets in the second key sequence, you get this:

It is often useful to know that **dividing by the product of several numbers is equivalent to dividing by each one in turn**.

For example, $\dfrac{120}{2 \times 3 \times 4}$ is equal to $120 \; \boxed{\div 2} \; \boxed{\div 3} \; \boxed{\div 4} \ggg$. (Check this!)

C1 Use this method to calculate   (a) $\dfrac{67 \cdot 6}{1 \cdot 3 \times 5 \cdot 2}$ (b) $\dfrac{7 \cdot 128}{16 \cdot 5 \times 0 \cdot 08 \times 4 \cdot 5}$

C2 s is given by the formula $s = \dfrac{vyz}{af}$.

    (a) Calculate s when $v = 1 \cdot 5, y = 0 \cdot 9, z = 2 \cdot 4, a = 16$ and $f = 0 \cdot 02$.
    (b) Re-arrange the formula to give z in terms of s, v, y, a and f.
    (c) Calculate z when $s = 84 \cdot 375, v = 12 \cdot 5, y = 18, a = 3 \cdot 2$ and $f = 0 \cdot 5$.

C3 The volume of a cone is given by the formula $V = \dfrac{\pi r^2 h}{3}$.

    V is the volume in cubic cm.
    r is the radius of the base, in cm.

    Calculate the height of a cone whose base radius is $5 \cdot 3$ cm and whose volume is 435 cubic cm.

D Further equations and re-arrangements

Look at this equation.
$$2{\cdot}6 = \frac{5{\cdot}46}{x}$$

The equation can be solved by first multiplying both sides by x.
$$2{\cdot}6x = 5{\cdot}46$$

Now divide both sides by $2{\cdot}6$.
$$x = \frac{5{\cdot}46}{2{\cdot}6} = 2{\cdot}1$$

> **D1** Solve these equations. Write out the working.
>
> (a) $4{\cdot}8 = \dfrac{5{\cdot}76}{x}$ (b) $15 = \dfrac{25{\cdot}5}{y}$ (c) $0{\cdot}99 = \dfrac{6{\cdot}93}{p}$

The method used in the next two examples of re-arrangement
is similar to the method used to solve the equations above.

Worked examples

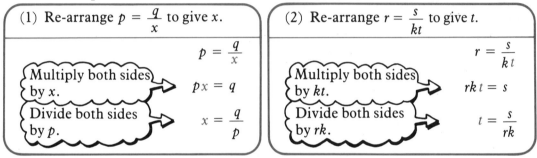

(1) Re-arrange $p = \dfrac{q}{x}$ to give x.

$$p = \frac{q}{x}$$

Multiply both sides by x. → $px = q$

Divide both sides by p. → $x = \dfrac{q}{p}$

(2) Re-arrange $r = \dfrac{s}{kt}$ to give t.

$$r = \frac{s}{kt}$$

Multiply both sides by kt. → $rkt = s$

Divide both sides by rk. → $t = \dfrac{s}{rk}$

In questions D2 to D4, re-arrange each formula to give the letter printed in red.

> **D2** (a) $l = \dfrac{m}{nz}$ (b) $a = \dfrac{be}{cx}$ (c) $f = \dfrac{A}{5n}$ (d) $u = \dfrac{ar}{t}$
>
> **D3** (a) $s = t + uvw$ (b) $s = t - uvw$ (c) $F = \dfrac{PT}{R}$
>
> (d) $m = \dfrac{l}{a} - b$ (e) $m = \dfrac{l}{a} - b$ (f) $q = \dfrac{5p}{q^2 b}$
>
> (g) $y = ab + \dfrac{x}{n}$ (h) $y = ab - \dfrac{x}{n}$ (i) $s = t - \dfrac{au}{bv}$
>
> ***D4** (a) $f = a(g + h)$ (Multiply out the brackets first.)
>
> (b) $m = p(q - r)$ (c) $d = a(b - c)$ (d) $h = fg(s - t)$
>
> (e) $d = \dfrac{a}{b+c}$ (Multiply both sides by $(b + c)$ first.
>   Then multiply out the brackets.)
>
> (f) $y = \dfrac{a}{b+x}$ (g) $y = \dfrac{a}{b-x}$ (h) $s = a - \dfrac{b}{r}$

97

6 Trigonometry (2)

6.1 Calculate the lengths marked with letters.

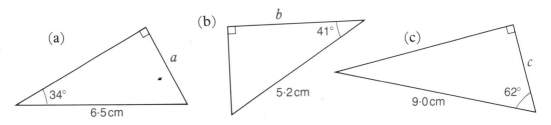

6.2 Calculate the lengths marked with letters.

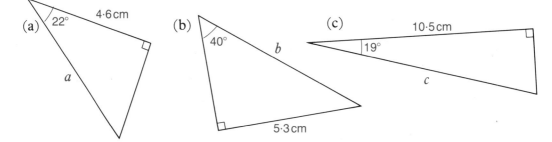

6.3 Calculate the angles marked with letters.

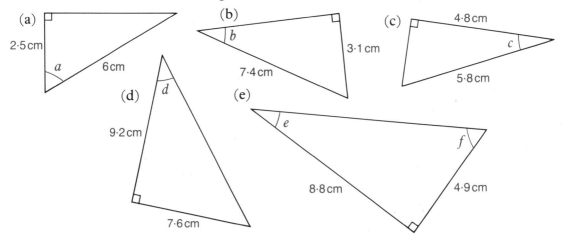

6.4 A ladder 4·5 m long leans against a vertical wall, the lower end of the ladder being on horizontal ground. The upper end is 3·8 m above the ground. Calculate the angle between the ladder and the ground.

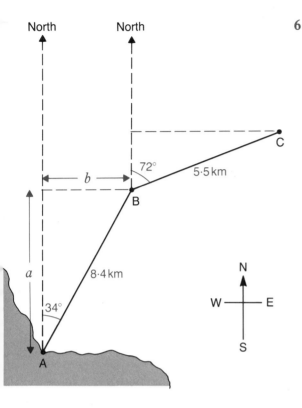

North   North

72°

5·5 km

C

b

B

N

W ——— E

S

a

8·4 km

34°

A

6.5 The map on the left shows the path of a motor boat.

For the first part of its journey, AB, it travelled on a bearing of 034° (34° clockwise from north) and covered 8·4 km.

For the second part of its journey, BC, it travelled on a bearing of 072° and covered 5·5 km.

(a) Calculate how far north of A is the point B. (This is the distance marked *a*.)

(b) Calculate how far east of A is the point B. (This is the distance marked *b*.)

(c) Calculate how far north of B is the point C.

(d) Calculate how far north of A is the point C.

(e) Calculate how far east of A is the point C.

6.6 A launch travelled from P to Q to R.
From P to Q it was on a bearing of 053°, and the distance PQ is 10·6 km.
From Q to R it was on a bearing of 022°, and the distance QR is 4·7 km.

Sketch the path of the launch.
Calculate how far   (a) north of P   (b) east of P is the point R.

6.7 Do question 6.6 again, but this time PQ is on a bearing of 063° and the distance PQ is 7·5 km; QR is on a bearing of 158° and the distance QR is 12·5 km.

6.8 The sides of a triangle have lengths 5 cm, 5 cm and 7 cm.
Calculate the angles of the triangle.

6.9 This diagram shows part of a circle, centre O, radius 14·5 cm.

A, B are two points on the circle, and the length of the line AB is 20·5 cm.

Calculate the angle AOB.

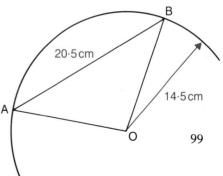

B

20·5 cm

A

14·5 cm

O

8.1 This timetable shows afternoon and evening trains from London (Fenchurch Street) to some places in South Essex.

Fenchurch Street	1500	1510	1530	1540	1600	....	1610	1630	1639	1650	1654	....	1700	1702	1704	1709	1715	1717	1719	....	1724	1730	1732	1734
Stepney East		1514		1544			1614		1643						1708				1723					1738
Barking	1512	1523		1553			1623		1652		1707				1717	1722			1732		1737		1747	
Upminster	1521	1532		1602	1619		1632		1701		1716				1726	1731			1741		1746		1756	
West Horndon		1537		1607			1637		1706						1731				1746					
Laindon		1542		1612			1643		1712	1717	1725		1729		1740		1744				1755		1759	
Basildon		1545	1557	1615			1646	1657	1715	1720			1732	1738		1747	1753					1802	1806
Pitsea		1549		1619			1650		1710	1723			1735	1742		1750	1757					1805	1810
Benfleet	1536	1553	1603	1623	1634		1654	1704	1722	1727		1733		1746		1749		1801		1804		1814
Leigh-on-Sea	1540	1557	1607	1627	1638		1658	1708	1727	1732		1738		1750		1754		1806		1809		1818
Chalkwell	1543	1600		1630	1641		1701	1711	1730	1735			1744	1753			1759	1809			1814	1821
Westcliff	1546	1603		1633	1644		1704	1714	1732	1737			1746	1756			1801	1811			1816	1824
Southend Central *arr.*	1547	1604	1612	1634	1645		1705	1715	1734	1739			1748	1757			1803	1813			1818	1825
Central *dep.*	1548	1605	1613	1635	1646		1706	1716	1735	1740			1749	1758			1804	1814			1819	1826
Southend East	1550	1607		1637	1648		1708	1718	1737	1742			1751	1800			1806	1816			1821	1828
Thorpe Bay	1553	1610	1616	1640	1651		1711	1721	1739	1744			1753	1803			1808	1818			1823	1832
Shoeburyness	1557	1614	1620	1644	1655		1715	1725	1743	1748			1757				1812	1823			1827	

Fenchurch Street	1739	1745	1747	1749	1754	1800	1802	1804	1809	....	1817	1819	....	1832	1834	1845	1900	1910	....	1930	1940	2000	2010	2030	2040
Stepney East				1753				1808				1823			1838	1849		1914			1944			2014	2044
Barking	1752		1802	1807			1817	1822				1832			1847	1858	1912	1923			1953	2012	2023		2053
Upminster	1801		1811	1816			1826	1831				1841		1851	1856	1907	1921	1932			2002	2021	2032		2102
West Horndon				1816								1846				1912		1937			2007		2037		2107
Laindon	1810		1814		1825		1829		1840			1852			1906	1917		1942		1957	2012		2042		2112
Basildon			1817	1823			1832	1836				1855			1906	1920		1945		1957	2015		2045	2057	2115
Pitsea			1820	1827			1835	1840				1858			1909	1924		1949			2019		2049		2119
Benfleet		1818		1831		1834		1844			1850	1902		1906	1913	1928	1936	1953		2003	2023	2036	2053	2103	2123
Leigh-on-Sea		1823		1836		1839		1848			1854	1907		1910	1918	1932	1940	1957		2007	2027	2040	2057	2107	2127
Chalkwell			1829	1839				1851			1857	1910		1913	1921	1935	1943	2000			2030	2043	2100		2130
Westcliff			1831	1841			1844	1854			1900	1912		1916	1923	1938	1946	2003			2033	2046	2103		2133
Southend Central *arr.*			1833	1843			1848	1855			1901	1914		1917	1925	1939	1947	2004		2012	2034	2047	2104	2112	2134
Central *dep.*			1834	1844			1849	1856			1902	1915		1918	1926	1940	1948	2005		2013	2035	2048	2105	2113	2135
Southend East			1836	1846			1851	1858			1904	1917		1920	1928	1942	1950	2007			2037	2050	2107		2137
Thorpe Bay			1838	1849			1853	1901			1907	1919		1923	1930	1945	1953	2010		2016	2040	2053	2110	2116	2140
Shoeburyness			1842				1857	1905			1911	1923		1927	1935	1949	1957	2014		2020	2044	2057	2114	2120	2144

Most of the trains, but not all, stop at Leigh-on-Sea.
Draw a frequency chart to show how many trains which stop at Leigh-on-Sea leave Fenchurch Street between 3 p.m. and 4 p.m., 4 p.m. and 5 p.m., 5 p.m. and 6 p.m., and so on up to 8 p.m.

8.2 (a) Work out the journey time in minutes for each train from Fenchurch Street to Leigh-on-Sea between 3 p.m. and 6 p.m. (include the 6 p.m. train). Make a frequency table like this.

Journey time in minutes	Tally	Frequency
35		
36		
etc.		

(b) Calculate the mean value of the journey times.
(c) Does the mean value give a good idea of a typical journey time? Give the reason for your answer.
(d) What is the range of the journey times?

8.3 Calculate the mean value of the number of letters in the words of this sentence.

8.4 Jamila counted the peas in a number of pea-pods. Her results are given below. Calculate the mean number of peas in a pod, to 1 d.p.

Number of peas in pod	3	4	5	6	7	8	9
Number of pods	2	5	8	13	15	6	3

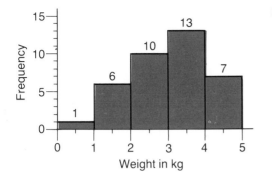

8.5 This chart shows the distribution of the weights of the babies born in a hospital during one month.

(a) Calculate an estimate of the mean weight of the babies.

(b) What percentage of the babies weighed under 2 kg?

9 Re-arranging formulas (1)

9.1 v, u, a and t are connected by the formula $v = u + at$.
(a) Calculate u, given that $v = 46 \cdot 3$, $a = 4 \cdot 2$, $t = 25$.
(b) Calculate a, given that $v = 60 \cdot 7$, $u = 21 \cdot 5$, $t = 30$.

9.2 p, q, r and s are connected by the formula $p = q - r + s$.
Make (a) q (b) s the subject of the formula.

9.3 In each case below, re-arrange the formula to give the letter printed in red.

(a) $y = at - b$ (b) $h = m + \dfrac{k}{n}$ (c) $s = \dfrac{u}{3} - a$

(d) $z = \dfrac{x}{a} + y$ (e) $d = p + uw$ (f) $w = k + \dfrac{x}{s}$

10 Points, lines and planes

10.1 ABCD is a piece of wire.
p is a plane sheet of paper.

Which of the points A, B, C and D are above the level of the plane p, and which are below it?

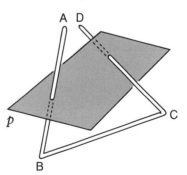

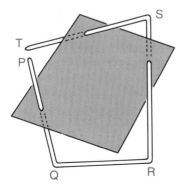

10.2 Explain why this is a picture of an impossible object.

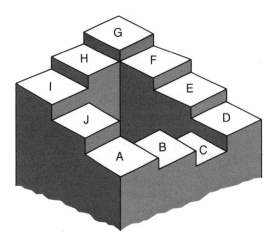

10.3 This is not an impossible object.

(a) Draw a view of the object looking down from above. Letter the squares in your view.

(b) Which of the 'steps' in the picture are not actually next to one another?

11 Re-arranging formulas (2)

11.1 Re-arrange each of these formulas to make the letter printed in red the subject of the formula.

(a) $p = qr - s$ (b) $p = qr - s$ (c) $d = a - bc$

(d) $t = \dfrac{u}{v} - w$ (e) $t = \dfrac{u}{v} - w$ (f) $h = f - \dfrac{g}{a}$

(g) $z = 3uxy$ (h) $r = \dfrac{2pq}{s}$ (i) $t = \dfrac{5a^2 b}{cd}$

11.2 Butchers once used the following formula to estimate how much meat could be obtained from a bullock's carcase.

$$w = \frac{5g^2 l}{21}$$

w is the weight of meat, in stones.
g is the girth of the bullock, in feet. (This is the circumference of its body, and is measured just behind its front legs.)
l is the length in feet from the shoulder to the rump.

(a) Calculate w when $g = 5 \cdot 8$ and $l = 4 \cdot 3$.
(b) Re-arrange the formula to give l in terms of w and g.
(c) Calculate l when $w = 38 \cdot 5$ and $g = 6 \cdot 2$.

M Miscellaneous

M1 How many different shapes can be made by sticking four identical cubes together, face to face?

Here are two shapes.

12 Proportionality

A The multiplier principle

(Before you start this chapter, remind yourself what the word 'proportional' means. Read again the explanation on page 8.)

Shadows

Imagine a pole which rises out of a hole in the ground.
It is 3 o'clock on a sunny day, and the pole casts a shadow.

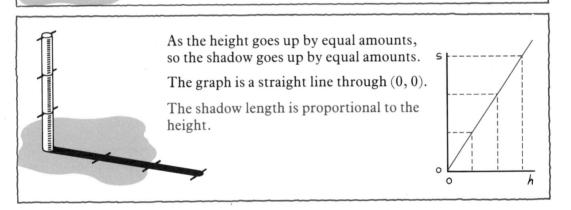

Suppose that the height, h, of the pole is 0 to start with.
The length, s, of the shadow is 0 as well.

So the graph of (h, s) goes through $(0, 0)$.

As the height goes up by equal amounts, so the shadow goes up by equal amounts.

The graph is a straight line through $(0, 0)$.

The shadow length is proportional to the height.

A1   On graph paper, draw axes with height h in metres marked across from 0 to 12, and shadow length s in metres marked up from 0 to 15.

At a particular time on a sunny afternoon, a pole 9·4 metres high casts a shadow 11·7 metres long.
(a) Mark the point $(9·4, 11·7)$ on the graph.
     Shadow length is proportional to height, so draw the graph of (h, s) as a straight line through $(0, 0)$ and $(9·4, 11·7)$.
(b) Use your graph to find s when h is   (i) 4·8   (ii) 11·8
(c) Find the height of a tree whose shadow is 10·8 metres long.

A2   If a pole of height 4 m casts a shadow 7 m long, how long will the shadow be of a pole whose height is   (a) 8 m   (b) 20 m

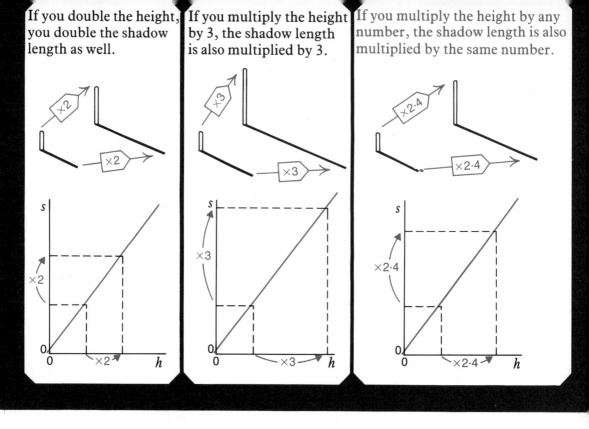

If you double the height, you double the shadow length as well.

If you multiply the height by 3, the shadow length is also multiplied by 3.

If you multiply the height by any number, the shadow length is also multiplied by the same number.

The 'multiplier principle' printed in red above can be used to calculate heights and shadow lengths.

For example, suppose that a pole of height 5·3 m casts a shadow 4·7 m long, and we want to calculate the shadow length for a pole of height 8·2 m.

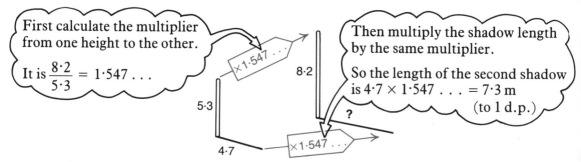

First calculate the multiplier from one height to the other.

It is $\dfrac{8 \cdot 2}{5 \cdot 3} = 1 \cdot 547 \ldots$

Then multiply the shadow length by the same multiplier.

So the length of the second shadow is $4 \cdot 7 \times 1 \cdot 547 \ldots = 7 \cdot 3$ m (to 1 d.p.)

A3   If a post 156 cm tall casts a shadow 234 cm long, calculate the length of the shadow of a post 324 cm long.

A4   If a tree 10·8 m tall casts a shadow of length 26·5 m, calculate the length of the shadow of a tree 14·2 m tall (to 1 d.p.)

A5   If a post 2·6 m tall has a shadow 7·1 m long, what is the height of a tree whose shadow is 45·3 m long? (Start by calculating the multiplier from the first shadow length to the second.)

The multiplier principle is true whenever one variable is proportional to another variable.

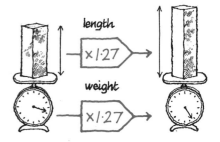

length

weight

For example, the weight of a uniform metal bar is proportional to its length. If you multiply the length by a number, then the weight is multiplied by the same number.

If q is proportional to p, then when you multiply a value of p by a number, the value of q is multiplied by the same number.

A6 Water is being poured into a cylinder.
When the depth of the water is 53·2 cm, the volume is 173·1 cubic cm.
What is the volume when the depth is 85·5 cm? (Start by calculating the multiplier from the first depth to the second.)

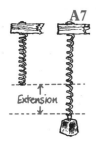

Extension

A7 When a weight is hung on the end of a spring, the spring extends. Hooke's law says that the amount of extension is proportional to the weight hung on the spring.

When a weight of 35 grams is hung on a certain spring, the spring extends by 9·3 cm. The weight of 35 grams is then taken off and replaced by a weight of 48 grams. By how much does the spring extend this time?

A8 q is proportional to p. When p is 408, q is 456.
What is q when p is 524 (to the nearest whole number)?

The multipliers in a proportionality calculation can be less than 1.

Suppose q is proportional to p, and q is 48·0 when p is 33·0, and we want to calculate q when p is 19·5.

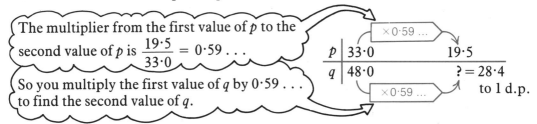

The multiplier from the first value of p to the second value of p is $\dfrac{19\cdot5}{33\cdot0} = 0\cdot59\ldots$

So you multiply the first value of q by $0\cdot59\ldots$ to find the second value of q.

$\times 0\cdot59\ldots$

p	33·0	19·5
q	48·0	? = 28·4

to 1 d.p.

$\times 0\cdot59\ldots$

A9 q is proportional to p. When p is 17·5, q is 59·2.
Calculate q when p is 12·5.

A10 In each table below, q is proportional to p.
Calculate the missing value of q or p in each case (to 1 d.p.)

(a)
p	7·0	5·0
q	9·6	?

(b)
p	8·3	6·7
q	5·9	?

(c)
p	12·3	16·6
q	4·7	?

(d)
p	6·1	?
q	2·8	9·5

(e)
p	14·8	?
q	6·5	3·5

(f)
p	7·6	?
q	10·2	8·7

B Non-proportionality

The multiplier principle only works when one variable is proportional to another.

B1 Let s cm be the length of one side of a square.
Let A sq cm be the area of the square.

(a) Copy and complete this table of values.

s	0	1	2	3	4	5	6
A							

(b) Draw a graph of (s, A).
Suitable scales are shown here.

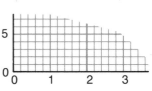

(c) Is A proportional to s?
(d) When s is 3, A is 9. What happens to A when s is doubled?
Is A doubled as well?

B2 This table shows the prices of various bags of peat at a garden centre.

Quantity in kg	5	10	15	30	40	50
Price in £	2·00	3·60	5·20	8·40	9·60	10·40

(a) 15 kg is 3 times as much as 5 kg.
Does 15 kg cost 3 times as much as 5 kg?
(b) Does 50 kg cost 10 times as much as 5 kg?
(c) Does 40 kg cost 4 times as much as 10 kg?
(d) Draw a graph of (quantity, cost).
Why is it sensible to make the graph go through $(0, 0)$?
(e) Is the cost proportional to the quantity?
How can you tell from the graph?

The garden centre decides to keep the same price for 30 kg of peat and then to make all prices proportional to quantity.

(f) On the same axes as before, draw a graph which shows how the new prices are related to quantities.
(g) Use your graph to make a new table of prices for the same quantities as in the table above.
(h) Check that when a quantity is doubled its (new) price is also doubled.

B3 How can you tell by just looking at this table that q is not proportional to p?

p	1·72	2·38	7·61	19·58	57·64	76·10	84·70
q	10·05	12·03	27·72	63·63	177·81	233·19	258·99

C Proportionality and gradient

We have seen that the length of an object's shadow is proportional to the height of the object.

This graph shows the relationship between shadow length and height at a particular time of day.
h stands for height in metres, and s stands for shadow length in metres.

The graph is a straight line so we can calculate its **gradient**. Because the line goes through $(0, 0)$ we can do this by choosing any point on the graph and using the values of s and h at that point.

The gradient of the graph is the ratio $\frac{s}{h}$.

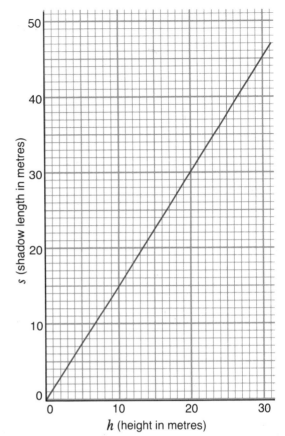

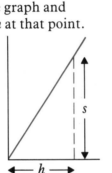

C1 (a) From the graph above, find the value of s when h is 20.
(b) Use these values of s and h to calculate the gradient of the graph.
(c) What is s when h is 30?
(d) Use these values of s and h to calculate the gradient.
(e) Calculate the gradient using the values of s and h at the point where s is 18.

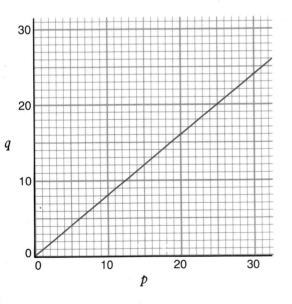

C2 A variable q is proportional to another variable p, and this graph shows the relationship between q and p.

(a) What is q when p is 20?
(b) Use these values of p and q to calculate the gradient of the graph.
(c) Calculate the gradient using the values of p and q at the point where p is 15.
(d) Choose another pair of values of p and q and calculate the gradient.

107

If a variable q is proportional to another variable p,

then the ratio $\frac{q}{p}$ is the same for every pair of values of p and q,

and this ratio is equal to the gradient of the graph of (p, q).

This is only true when q is proportional to p, that is, when the graph of (p, q) is a straight line through $(0,0)$.

C3 Here is a case in which q is not proportional to p, because the graph is not a straight line, even though it goes through $(0, 0)$.

Calculate the ratio $\frac{q}{p}$ at each of the marked points. You should find that the ratios are not all equal.

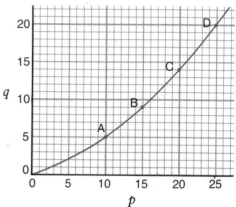

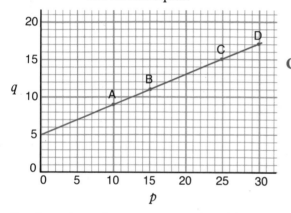

C4 Here is another case in which q is not proportional to p. (Although the graph is a straight line, it does not go through $(0, 0)$.)

Calculate the ratio $\frac{q}{p}$ at each of the marked points.

Look again at the statement printed in red at the top of this page. If we have some values of two variables p and q, we can use the first part of the statement to test if q is proportional to p. We calculate the values of $\frac{q}{p}$. If they are all equal, q is proportional to p; otherwise not.

C5 (a) Copy and complete this table.

(b) Is q proportional to p?

p	550	635	725	880	1210
q	770	886	1015	1408	1815
$\frac{q}{p}$					

C6 An electrician made these measurements of the current, I amps, and the voltage, V volts, of an electrical component.

I	3·6	4·0	5·8	7·2	10·4	18·2
V	30·6	34·0	49·3	61·2	88·4	154·7

Is V proportional to I?

D Proportionality and equations

This graph shows the relationship between two variables p and q. You can see from the graph that q is proportional to p.

The gradient of the graph can be calculated by using the values of p and q at any point on it. For example, if we choose the point A, whose coordinates are (20, 36), we find that the

gradient is $\dfrac{36}{20} = \mathbf{1 \cdot 8}$

So at every point on the graph, the value of $\dfrac{q}{p}$ is $1 \cdot 8$.

So the relationship between q and p can be written $\quad \dfrac{q}{p} = 1 \cdot 8$.

If we multiply both sides of this equation by p, we get $\quad q = 1 \cdot 8p$.

This is the most useful form of the equation which connects q and p.

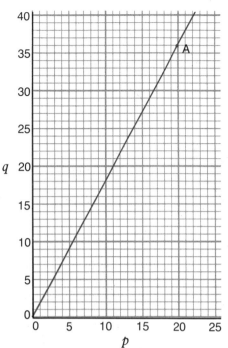

D1 For each of the graphs below, do this.
(i) Find the gradient of the graph.
(ii) Write the equation connecting q and p in the form $q = \ldots p$.
(iii) Calculate q when $p = 200$.

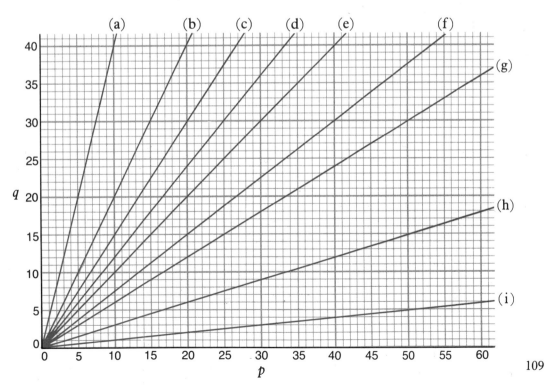

D2 These pictures are all enlargements of one another.

(a) Measure in millimetres the short side, s, and the long side, l, of each picture.
Make a table.

s	
l	

(b) Draw a graph of (s, l).
(c) Is l proportional to s?
(d) Find the gradient of the graph.
(e) Write the equation connecting l and s in the form $l = \ldots s$.

D3 These rectangles are all similar to one another, except for one, which is an 'odd one out'.

(a) Measure the short side, s, and the long side, l, of each rectangle. Make a table of values of s and l.

(b) Draw axes on graph paper, and plot each pair of values as a point. Which rectangle is the 'odd one out'?

(c) Draw the straight line which goes through $(0, 0)$ and the other three points. Find its gradient and write its equation in the form $l = \ldots s$.

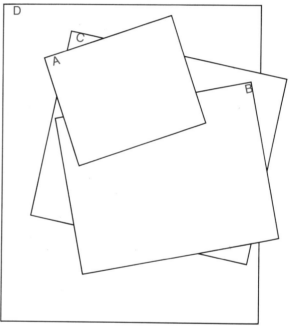

(d) What is the value of $\dfrac{l}{s}$ for the rectangle which is the 'odd one out'?

D4 The length and mass of six pieces of copper wire were measured.
Here are the results.

l (length in mm)	20	25	35	55	60	85
m (mass in grams)	44	40	77	88	132	136

The pieces of wire came from two different rolls of wire.
(a) Draw axes and plot the six pairs of values. Each point lies on one of two straight lines through $(0, 0)$. Draw the lines.
(b) Find the equation of each line. Which one represents the thicker wire?

E Approximate proportionality

Different masses were hung on a spring, and the extension was measured each time. (The extension is the amount the spring stretches from its original length.)

Here are the results. m stands for the mass in grams, e for the extension in mm.

m	50	100	150	200	250	300
e	80	180	250	350	435	500

When these measurements are plotted, the points do not lie exactly on a straight line through $(0, 0)$.
So e is not exactly proportional to m.

But the points are all very close to the dotted line shown here. This line has been drawn so that it goes through $(0, 0)$ and 'through the middle' of the group of six marked points. Some of the marked points are slightly above the line and some slightly below it.

(The position of the line has to be judged 'by eye'. This means that different people might draw slightly different lines.)

The line's gradient is $1 \cdot 7$. (You can work it out from the fact that it goes through $(300, 510)$ and $\dfrac{510}{300} = 1 \cdot 7$.)

So the equation of the line is $e = 1 \cdot 7\,m$.

The measurements in the table do not fit the equation $e = 1 \cdot 7\,m$ exactly, but they fit it roughly. Experimental measurements can never be expected to fit a rule exactly.

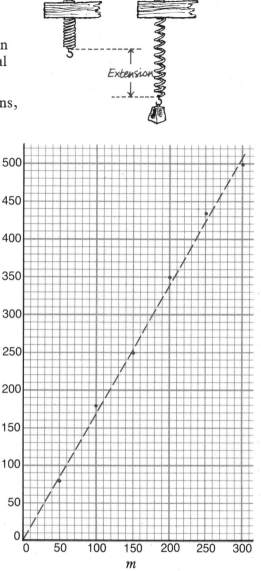

E1 (a) Calculate $\dfrac{e}{m}$, to 2 d.p., for each pair of values in the table above.

   (b) How many values of $\dfrac{e}{m}$ are greater than $1 \cdot 7$, and how many are less?

E2 These values of m and e were obtained with a different spring.

m	50	100	150	200	250	300
e	60	140	190	270	320	400

   (a) Draw axes and plot the six pairs of values.
   (b) Draw a straight line through $(0, 0)$ so that all six points are close to it or on it.
   (c) Calculate the gradient of your line, and write its equation.

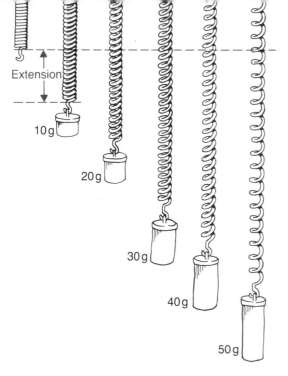

Extension

10g

20g

30g

40g

50g

E3 These diagrams are all full-size. They show the same spring with different weights on it.

(a) Measure in mm the extension of the spring in each diagram. Make a table of values of m and e.

(b) Draw axes and plot the values of m and e from your table. Draw the line through $(0, 0)$ which seems to you to 'fit' the points most closely.

(c) Calculate the gradient of your line and write down its equation.

E4 These values of two variables P and Q were obtained in an experiment.

P	1·5	2·1	2·7	3·4	4·0	5·0
Q	0·4	1·5	2·4	3·5	4·6	6·1

(a) Draw axes and plot the values of P and Q.

(b) Is Q approximately proportional to P? If so, what equation do P and Q fit roughly?

*E5 A student carrying out an experiment in electricity passed an electric current through a piece of copper wire. She varied the voltage across the ends of the wire and each time measured the current in the wire. (Voltage is measured in volts and current in amps.)

Here are her results.

Voltage (volts)	1·25	2·19	2·94	3·60	4·06
Current (amps)	1·05	1·86	2·43	2·92	3·41

(a) Draw a graph of (voltage, current).

(b) Is the current approximately proportional to the voltage?

(c) If V stands for the voltage and I for the current, the relationship between V and I is usually written in the form $V = IR$, where the number R is called the resistance of the wire (measured in ohms). Calculate a value for R in this case.

13 Area

A The area of a parallelogram

P is a parallelogram.
It stands on a 'base' of length b.
Its height, measured at right-angles to
the base, is h.

Enclose the parallelogram in a
rectangle, like this.
The rectangle is made up of two
right-angled triangles A and B,
and the parallelogram P.

   Area of red rectangle $= P + A + B$.

Slide triangle A to the right, like this.
Now the same red rectangle is made up
of A, B and the rectangle R. So

   Area of red rectangle $= R + A + B$.

So P must have the same area as R.
So the area of P is equal to bh.

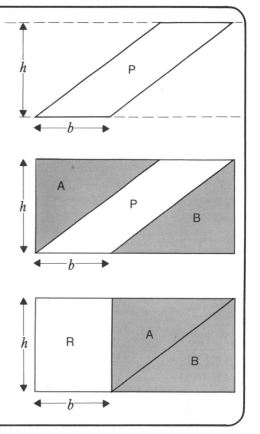

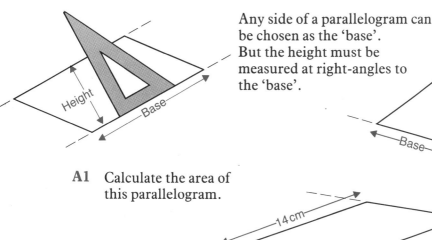

Any side of a parallelogram can
be chosen as the 'base'.
But the height must be
measured at right-angles to
the 'base'.

A1 Calculate the area of
this parallelogram.

A2 (a) Think of AB as the base of this parallelogram. Measure the base and the height. Calculate the area to the nearest $0 \cdot 1 \, \text{cm}^2$. (cm^2 means 'square centimetre'.)

(b) Do the same, but this time think of BC as the base.

A3 (a) Calculate the area, in square units, of the parallelogram PQRS.

(b) Calculate the area of the parallelogram with corners at $(^-3, \, ^-3)$, $(2, 4)$, $(4, 4)$ and $(^-1, \, ^-3)$.

(c) Calculate the area of the parallelogram with corners at $(^-2, 4)$, $(^-2, \, ^-2)$, $(3, \, ^-3)$ and $(3, 3)$.

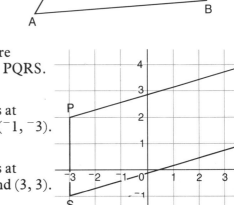

A4 Find the area of the printed part of this stamp, in cm^2 (to the nearest $0 \cdot 1 \, \text{cm}^2$).

A5 Calculate the area of this shape.

A6 Calculate the distance marked d. (**Hint.** Calculate the area first.)

114

B The area of a triangle

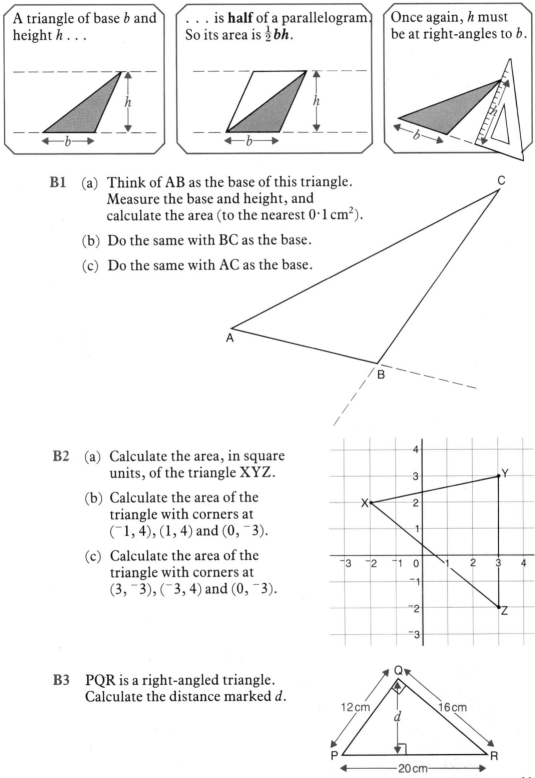

A triangle of base b and height h . . .

. . . is **half** of a parallelogram. So its area is $\frac{1}{2}bh$.

Once again, h must be at right-angles to b.

B1 (a) Think of AB as the base of this triangle. Measure the base and height, and calculate the area (to the nearest $0 \cdot 1 \, \text{cm}^2$).

(b) Do the same with BC as the base.

(c) Do the same with AC as the base.

B2 (a) Calculate the area, in square units, of the triangle XYZ.

(b) Calculate the area of the triangle with corners at $(^-1, 4)$, $(1, 4)$ and $(0, ^-3)$.

(c) Calculate the area of the triangle with corners at $(3, ^-3)$, $(^-3, 4)$ and $(0, ^-3)$.

B3 PQR is a right-angled triangle. Calculate the distance marked d.

12 cm   16 cm

d

P

20 cm

R

C The area of a trapezium

A **quadrilateral** is a 4-sided shape.

A **trapezium** is a quadrilateral with
two of its sides parallel to each other.

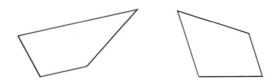

C1 Which of these shapes are trapeziums?

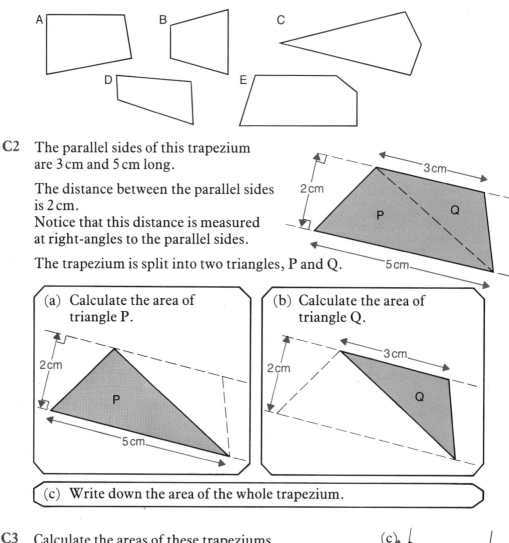

C2 The parallel sides of this trapezium
are 3 cm and 5 cm long.

The distance between the parallel sides
is 2 cm.
Notice that this distance is measured
at right-angles to the parallel sides.

The trapezium is split into two triangles, P and Q.

(a) Calculate the area of
triangle P.

(b) Calculate the area of
triangle Q.

(c) Write down the area of the whole trapezium.

C3 Calculate the areas of these trapeziums.
(Dimensions are in centimetres.)

(a)

(b)

(c)

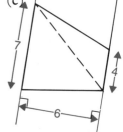

Let a, b be the lengths of the parallel sides of a trapezium.
Let h be the distance between the two parallel sides
(h must be measured at right-angles to the parallel sides).

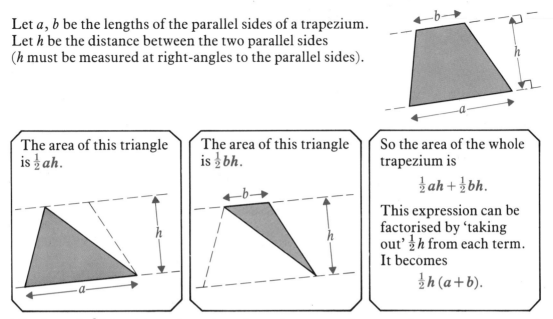

The area of this triangle is $\frac{1}{2}ah$.

The area of this triangle is $\frac{1}{2}bh$.

So the area of the whole trapezium is

$$\frac{1}{2}ah + \frac{1}{2}bh.$$

This expression can be factorised by 'taking out' $\frac{1}{2}h$ from each term. It becomes

$$\frac{1}{2}h(a+b).$$

The formula $\frac{1}{2}h(a+b)$ can be written in various ways; for example,

$$\frac{h(a+b)}{2} \qquad \frac{(a+b)h}{2} \qquad \frac{1}{2}(a+b)h \qquad \left(\frac{a+b}{2}\right)h$$

C4 Use the formula $\frac{1}{2}h(a+b)$ to calculate the area of a trapezium. when a is 5, b is 3 and h is 10.

Check that the other four formulas above all give the same result.

The last formula in the list above can be 'translated' into words, like this.

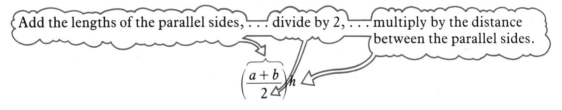

Add the lengths of the parallel sides, ⋯ divide by 2, ⋯ multiply by the distance between the parallel sides.

$$\left(\frac{a+b}{2}\right)h$$

This is a simple way to remember the rule for finding the area of a trapezium.

C5 Use the rule to calculate the areas of these trapeziums.

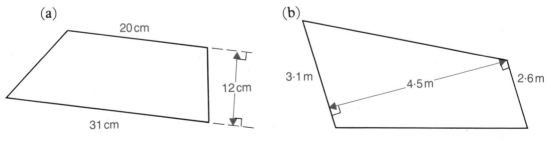

(a)
20 cm
12 cm
31 cm

(b)
3·1 m
4·5 m
2·6 m

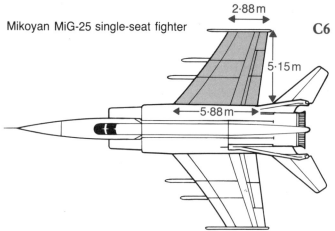

Mikoyan MiG-25 single-seat fighter

C6 Use the information given here to get an estimate of the area of the top of the MiG's wing, to the nearest $0 \cdot 1\,m^2$.

C7 This is a drawing of the end wall of a factory.

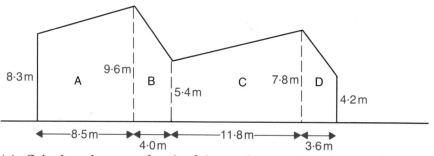

(a) Calculate the area of each of the sections marked A, B, C, D.

(b) Calculate the total area of the wall.

(c) Calculate the cost of providing heat insulation for this wall at a rate of £6·50 per square metre.

C8 Find the area of the top of this aircraft's wing, to the nearest $0 \cdot 1\,m^2$.

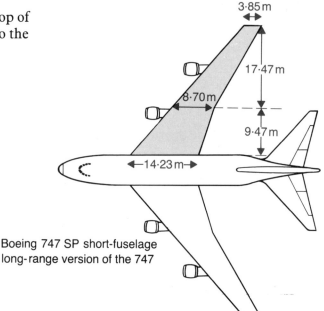

Boeing 747 SP short-fuselage long-range version of the 747

An offset survey

For many centuries, probably since farming first began, there have been disputes about who owned pieces of land. So people made maps and plans, as accurately as they could, to show who owned what. When a piece of land was exchanged, or bought and sold, it was necessary to know its area.

Making measurements of a piece of land, and drawing a plan from them, is called **surveying**. There are many different methods of surveying; one of them, described here, is called the **offset** method.

This is how a field is surveyed by the offset method.

C9   Here is a sketch-plan of the field.
The numbers marked in red are the offsets, in metres.
The numbers marked in black are distances along the base line, in metres.

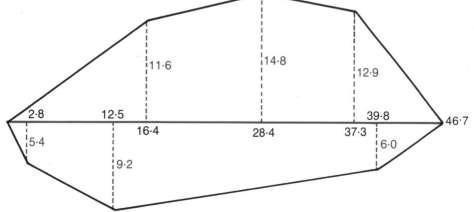

Calculate the area of the field, to the nearest square metre.

D Regular polygons and circles

Inside any regular polygon you can draw a circle which touches every side of the polygon.

The circle is called the **inscribed circle** of the polygon. Its radius is called the **inscribed radius** of the polygon.

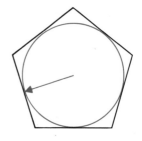

A regular polygon can be 'opened out' into triangles, like this.

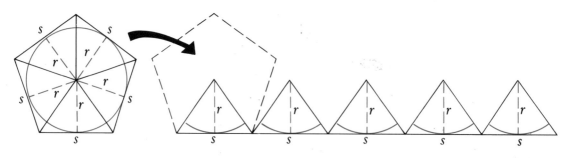

The base of each triangle is a side, s, of the polygon. The height of each triangle is the inscribed radius, r.

The area of each triangle is $\frac{1}{2}sr$.

So the total area is $\frac{1}{2}sr \times n$, where n is the number of sides of the polygon. (n is 5 in the diagram above.)

Now $\frac{1}{2}sr \times n = \frac{1}{2}srn = \frac{1}{2}nsr$.

But ns is the perimeter of the polygon. (It is $5s$ in the diagram.)

So the total area $= \frac{1}{2}$ **perimeter** $\times r$.

D1 Calculate (i) the perimeter (ii) the area of each of these regular polygons. (The lengths are in centimetres.)

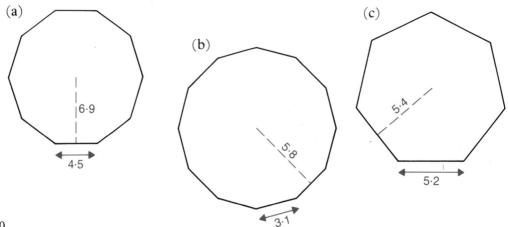

(a) 6·9, 4·5

(b) 5·8, 3·1

(c) 5·4, 5·2

A regular polygon with a very large number of sides is almost indistinguishable from a circle.

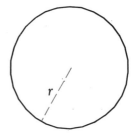

We can think of a circle as a regular polygon with an enormous number of very short sides.

The inscribed radius of a circle will be its own radius.

If the radius is r, the diameter is $2r$.
The perimeter, or circumference, is $\pi \times \text{diameter} = \pi \times 2r = 2\pi r$.
So the area is $\frac{1}{2}$ perimeter $\times r$

$$= \tfrac{1}{2} \times 2\pi r \times r$$

$$= \quad \pi r \quad \times r \quad \text{(because } \tfrac{1}{2} \times 2 = 1\text{)}$$

$$= \pi r^2.$$

Note that πr^2 means $\pi \times r \times r$, just as $3a^2$ means $3 \times a \times a$.
πr^2 means 'π times (r-squared)', **not** '(π-times-r) squared'.

When you use a calculator to work out πr^2, it is best to do it like this.

$$\boxed{\text{Enter } r} \text{——} \boxed{\text{Square}} \text{——} \boxed{\text{Multiply by } \pi}$$

D2 Calculate (to the nearest $0 \cdot 1 \, \text{m}^2$) the area of a circle whose radius is
    (a) $5 \cdot 0 \, \text{m}$ (b) $6 \cdot 7 \, \text{m}$ (c) $13 \cdot 5 \, \text{m}$ (d) $31 \cdot 4 \, \text{m}$ (e) $200 \, \text{m}$

Do not confuse the formulas for the area and for the circumference.

        Circumference $= 2\pi r$
            Area $= \pi r^2$

> The squaring symbol should remind you that this is the **area** formula, because area is measured in square units.

D3 Calculate (a) the circumference (b) the area of a circle whose radius is $4 \cdot 8 \, \text{m}$, each to 2 significant figures.

D4 The diameter of a circle is $13 \cdot 6 \, \text{cm}$.
Calculate (a) the circumference (b) the area of the circle to 3 significant figures.

D5 Calculate the area of each of these shapes.

(a)   (b)   (c)

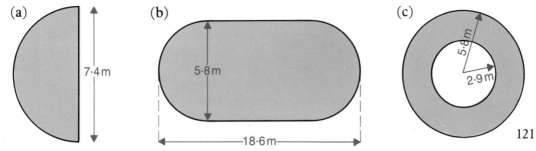

121

E Calculating the radius of a circle

If the area of a circle is 40 cm², we can calculate the radius like this:

Let r cm be the radius. Then $\pi r^2 = 40$.
So we now have an equation to solve.

We cannot find r directly, but we can find r^2, like this.

Divide both sides of the equation by π. $\quad \dfrac{\pi r^2}{\pi} = \dfrac{40}{\pi}$

$$\text{So} \quad r^2 = \frac{40}{\pi} = \frac{40}{3\cdot 14 \ldots} = 12\cdot 73 \ldots$$

If r^2 is $12\cdot 73 \ldots$, then r itself must be the square root of $12\cdot 73 \ldots$

$$\text{So} \quad r = \sqrt{12\cdot 73 \ldots} = \mathbf{3\cdot 57}, \text{ to 3 s.f.}$$

E1 A circle has an area of $12\cdot 5$ cm².
Let its radius be r cm.
Calculate r by solving the equation $\pi r^2 = 12\cdot 5$.

E2 Do the same as in question E1 for a circle of area $19\cdot 2$ cm².

E3 A square and a circle have the same area.
The square has sides each 5 cm long.
Calculate the radius of the circle, to the nearest $0\cdot 1$ cm.

E4 The coloured area is half of the area
of the square in this diagram.

Calculate the radius of the circle,
to the nearest $0\cdot 1$ cm.

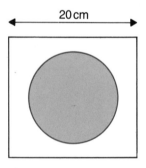

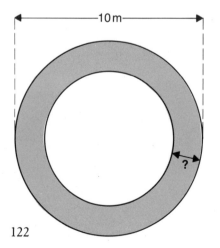

E5 The outer circle in this diagram has a
diameter of 10 m.

The area of the inner circle is half
of the area of the outer circle.

(a) First have a guess at the width of the
ring.

(b) Calculate the width of the ring,
to 3 significant figures.

14 Linear equations and inequalities

A Equations and inequalities

Printers classify the shapes of books into three types.
Let h stand for the height of a book and w for the width.

A book is called 'portrait' shape if h is greater than w.	It is called 'square' if h is equal to w.	It is called 'landscape' shape if h is less than w.

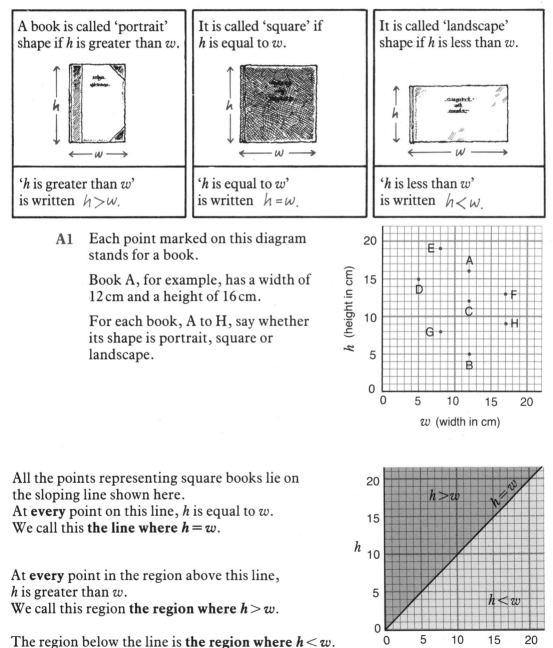

'h is greater than w' is written $h > w$.

'h is equal to w' is written $h = w$.

'h is less than w' is written $h < w$.

A1 Each point marked on this diagram stands for a book.

Book A, for example, has a width of 12 cm and a height of 16 cm.

For each book, A to H, say whether its shape is portrait, square or landscape.

All the points representing square books lie on the sloping line shown here.
At **every** point on this line, h is equal to w.
We call this **the line where $h = w$**.

At **every** point in the region above this line, h is greater than w.
We call this region **the region where $h > w$**.

The region below the line is **the region where $h < w$**.

123

Statements with an '=' sign in them are called **equations**.
Statements with a '>' or '<' sign in them are called **inequalities**.

A2 Each red number on this grid
shows the value of $x + y$ at
the point where it is written.

For example, at the point $(0, 5)$
x is 0 and y is 5, so $x + y$ is 5.

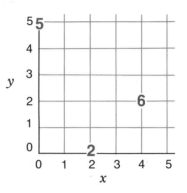

(a) Draw the grid and write the
value of $x + y$ at every grid point
(every point with whole-number
coordinates).

(b) You should find that the points where $x + y = 4$ lie on a line.
Draw the line.
What inequality is true at all points **below** the line?

(c) What inequality is true at all points **above** the line?

A3 Draw a grid as before. This time write the value of $x - y$ at
each grid point. ($x - y$ will be negative at some points.)

Draw the line through the points where $x - y = 2$.

(a) What inequality is true at all points below the line?
(b) What inequality is true at all points above the line?

A4 Draw a grid as before. Write the value of $2x + y$ at each
grid point. Draw the line through the points where $2x + y = 4$.

What inequality is true at all points (a) below (b) above the line?

A5 This diagram shows the line
where $y = 2x$.

It goes through $(3, 6)$ for example,
because 6 is 2×3.

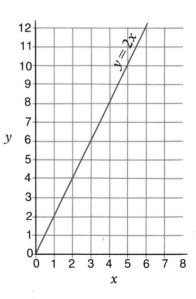

(a) Pick a few points in the region
above the line.
At each point see whether y is
greater than $2x$ or less than $2x$.

What inequality is true at all
points in the region above the line?

(b) What inequality is true at all
points below the line?

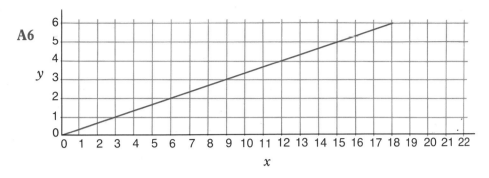

A6

(a) What equation is true at all points on the sloping line?
(b) What inequality is true at all points below the line?
(c) What inequality is true at all points above the line?

B Mixtures

A factory supplies cement in 2 kg bags and 5 kg bags.
Do-it-yourself shops send in orders for cement, and each order
can be any mixture of the two sizes, for example, 10 small
and 3 large.

We can record on a grid the weights of all the possible mixtures.

Let the number of small bags be x,
and the number of large bags be y.

Each point with whole number coordinates
(including zeros) stands for a possible mixture.
For example, the point $(4, 3)$ means '4 small
and 3 large'. The total weight of this mixture
is $4 \times 2\,\text{kg} + 3 \times 5\,\text{kg} = 23\,\text{kg}$.

We can write the weight of each mixture at
its grid point.

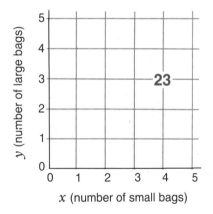

B1 Draw the grid with x and y from 0 to 5.
Mark the weight of each mixture at its grid point.

What you have just done can be described in the language of algebra.
If the mixture is $(4, 3)$ its weight is $4 \times 2\,\text{kg} + 3 \times 5\,\text{kg}$.
If the mixture is $(3, 2)$ its weight is $3 \times 2\,\text{kg} + 2 \times 5\,\text{kg}$.
If the mixture is (x, y) its weight is $x \times 2\,\text{kg} + y \times 5\,\text{kg}$
            or $2x$ $+$ $5y$ kilograms

At each grid point you have written the value of $2x + 5y$ at that point.
Make sure you understand this before you go any further.

The grid you have drawn is part of this larger one.
The red numbers show values of $2x + 5y$ at each grid point.

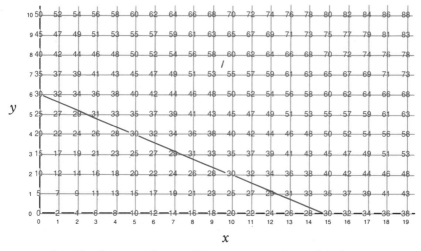

Suppose now that the factory gives a discount on orders of 30 kg or more.
There are four mixtures whose weight is exactly 30 kg. They are

(0, 6), (5, 4), (10, 2) (15, 0).

These points are in a straight line.

Notice that at every grid point **above** the line, the weight is **greater**
than 30 kg, and at every point **below** the line, the weight is **less** than 30 kg.

Remember that the weight at any point is the value of $2x + 5y$
at that point. So we can say that

the region **above** the line is **the region where $2x + 5y > 30$**,
the region **below** the line is **the region where $2x + 5y < 30$**.

If we now rub out the red numbers and just leave the line in position,
we have a graph which can be used to tell immediately whether an order
qualifies for a discount.

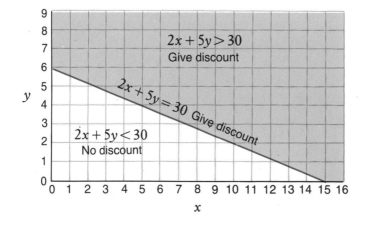

Use the graph at the bottom of the opposite page to answer
questions B2 to B4.

B2 Which of these mixtures qualifies for a discount?
(a) $(9, 3)$ (b) $(6, 3)$ (c) $(13, 1)$ (d) $(11, 8)$ (e) $(4, 4)$

B3 A shop orders 7 small bags (so x is 7). What is the smallest
number of large bags it must order to get a discount?

B4 A shop orders 4 large bags (so y is 4). What is the smallest
number of small bags it must order to get a discount?

B5 On squared paper draw axes with x and y from 0 to 10.
Find as many points as you can where $2x + 3y = 18$.
Draw the line which goes through all of these points.

Time-saving

Suppose you want to draw the graph of $2x + 5y = 20$.
You could work out $2x + 5y$ at different grid points until you find
some points where $2x + 5y = 20$.

This may take a long time. There is a much quicker way to draw the
graph if you know it is going to be a straight line.
(All the graphs in this chapter will be straight lines.)

To draw a line you need to know only **two** points on it.
The easiest points to find are the points where the line crosses the axes.
This is how you do it for the equation $2x + 5y = 20$.

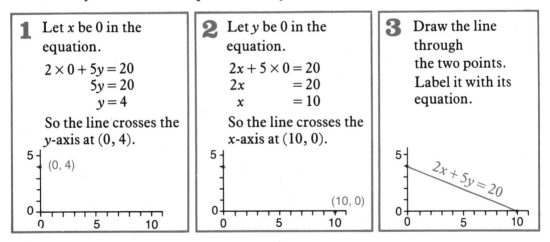

1 Let x be 0 in the equation.

$2 \times 0 + 5y = 20$
$5y = 20$
$y = 4$

So the line crosses the y-axis at $(0, 4)$.

2 Let y be 0 in the equation.

$2x + 5 \times 0 = 20$
$2x = 20$
$x = 10$

So the line crosses the x-axis at $(10, 0)$.

3 Draw the line through the two points. Label it with its equation.

B6 Draw axes with x and y from 0 to 15.
(a) Draw the line where $3x + 4y = 12$. Label the line.
(b) On the same axes, draw and label the line $3x + 4y = 24$.
(c) On the same axes, draw and label the line $3x + 4y = 36$.
(d) What do you notice about the three lines?
(e) Shade the region where $3x + 4y > 36$.

B7 Draw axes with x and y from 0 to 15.

On the same axes draw and label the lines with these equations.

$$3x + 2y = 12 \qquad 3x + 2y = 18 \qquad 3x + 2y = 27$$

(a) Shade the region where $3x + 2y < 12$.

(b) Without doing any calculation, draw a dotted line to show roughly where you think the line $3x + 2y = 20$ will be.

Isotherms: a comparison

Maps like these are used in meteorology (the study of the weather).

Each red line is called an **isotherm** (which means 'equal-heat'). The isotherm marked 12 °C goes through all the points whose temperature is 12 °C, and similarly for the other isotherms.

You can see from the map that the temperature gets higher as you go south.

The coloured region, south of the 14 °C isotherm is the region where the temperature is greater than 14 °C.

You may be wondering what this has got to do with graphs.

Look at this diagram showing the graphs of $2x + 3y = 18$, $2x + 3y = 12$, ... etc.

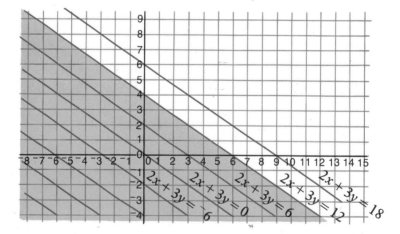

Each straight line is a kind of 'isotherm'. But instead of going through points where the temperature is the same, each one goes through points where the value of $2x + 3y$ is the same.

The shaded region is the region where $2x + 3y < 12$.

128

C Using straight-line graphs

A factory supplies oil in 2-litre tins and 3-litre tins.
They give a discount on orders of 18 litres or more.
They make a delivery charge on orders of less than 12 litres.

The problem is to draw a graph which will show whether an order
qualifies for a discount or not, and whether it will incur a delivery
charge or not.

The first step is to translate the information into the language of algebra.
Let x be the number of small tins, and y the number of large tins.
If you order x small tins and y large tins, the amount of oil you get
is $(x \times 2 \text{ litres}) + (y \times 3 \text{ litres}) = 2x + 3y$ litres.

So if $2x + 3y > 18$ $\Big\}$ the order qualifies for a discount.
or $2x + 3y = 18$

And if $2x + 3y < 12$, the order incurs a delivery charge.

The second step is to draw the two straight lines where $2x + 3y = 18$,
and where $2x + 3y = 12$.

The lines are shown in this diagram.
The regions where $2x + 3y > 18$ and
where $2x + 3y < 12$ are shown by shading.

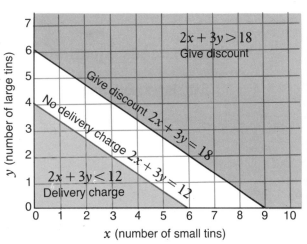

Any order actually on the line
$2x + 3y = 18$ does get a discount,
because a discount is given on
orders of 18 litres or more.

Any order on the line $2x + 3y = 12$
does not incur a delivery charge,
because the charge is made for
orders of less than 12 litres.

C1 Use the graph to find out if these orders qualify for a discount
or incur a delivery charge. (a) $(2, 3)$ (b) $(5, 3)$ (c) $(4, 1)$

C2 A garden centre sells fertilizer in 4 kg bags and 3 kg bags.
They give a discount on orders of 24 kg or more.

Suppose a customer orders x 4 kg bags and y 3 kg bags.
(a) Write down an expression for the total amount of
fertilizer in the order.
(b) Write down the equation which says 'the total amount
ordered is 24 kg'.
(c) On a graph, draw the line which has this equation.
Label the regions, and the line itself, 'discount' or 'no discount'.

129

C3 Oranges cost 8p each and apples 6p each.
A woman has up to 72p to spend on oranges and apples.

Suppose she orders x oranges and y apples.
(a) Write an expression for the total cost of her order.
(b) Write the equation which says 'the total cost of the order is 72p'.
(c) Draw on a graph the line which has this equation.
Shade the region containing all the orders which the woman cannot afford.

C4 In an athletics competition, an athlete gets 5 points for coming first in an event and 3 points for coming second.
At the end of the competition, athletes with more than 15 points but less than 30 get a silver medal. Those with 30 or more get a gold medal.

(a) If an athlete comes first x times and second y times, write an expression for the total number of points he or she scores.
(b) Write down the equation which says 'the total score is 15'.
(c) Write down the equation which says 'the total score is 30'.
(d) Draw on a graph the two lines which have these equations.
Label the regions and lines 'no medal', 'silver', 'gold'.

D Simultaneous equations

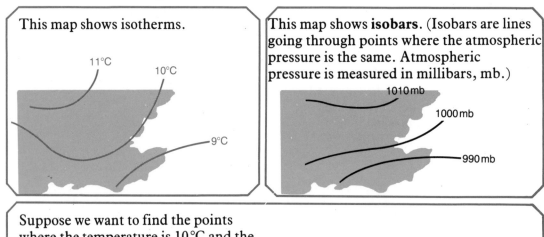

This map shows isotherms.

11°C
10°C
9°C

This map shows **isobars**. (Isobars are lines going through points where the atmospheric pressure is the same. Atmospheric pressure is measured in millibars, mb.)

1010mb
1000mb
990mb

Suppose we want to find the points where the temperature is 10°C and the atmospheric pressure is 1000mb.

We can do it by **superimposing** the two maps (putting one over the other).

We can see that the 10°C isotherm crosses the 1000mb isobar at two points P and Q. At each of these points, the temperature is 10°C and the pressure 1000mb.

11°C
1010mb
10°C
1000mb
P
Q
9°C
990mb

The same idea can be applied to graphs.

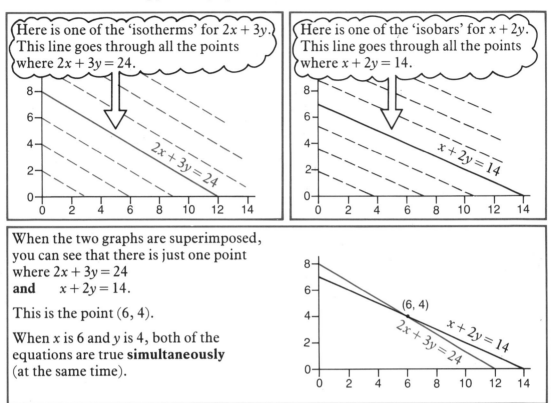

Here is one of the 'isotherms' for $2x + 3y$. This line goes through all the points where $2x + 3y = 24$.

Here is one of the 'isobars' for $x + 2y$. This line goes through all the points where $x + 2y = 14$.

$2x + 3y = 24$

$x + 2y = 14$

When the two graphs are superimposed, you can see that there is just one point where $2x + 3y = 24$
and $x + 2y = 14$.

This is the point $(6, 4)$.

When x is 6 and y is 4, both of the equations are true **simultaneously** (at the same time).

$(6, 4)$

$2x + 3y = 24$

$x + 2y = 14$

D1 Check that the values $x = 6$ and $y = 4$ fit both of the equations $2x + 3y = 24$ and $x + 2y = 14$ simultaneously.

D2 Draw axes with x and y from 0 to 10.
(a) Draw and label the graph of $3x + 2y = 18$.
(b) Draw and label the graph of $3x + 4y = 24$.
(c) What values of x and y fit both equations simultaneously?
(d) Check that these values do fit both equations.

D3 (a) Draw the graphs of $2x + 4y = 16$ and $5x + 2y = 20$ on the same axes.
(b) Find the values of x and y which fit both equations simultaneously.
(c) Check that the values do fit both equations.

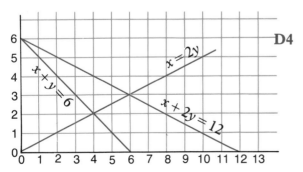

$x = 2y$

$x + y = 6$

$x + 2y = 12$

D4 Use the graph on the left to find the values of x and y which fit these pairs of equations simultaneously.

(a) $x + y = 6$, $\quad x + 2y = 12$

(b) $x = 2y$, $\quad x + 2y = 12$

(c) $x + y = 6$, $\quad x = 2y$

131

Up to now in this chapter no negative values of x and y have appeared, and we have not had equations like $2x - 5y = 15$.

To draw the graph of $2x - 5y = 15$, you do the same as before. You find where it crosses the axes.

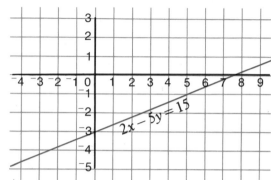

(1) When x is 0, then $^-5y = 15$
    so $y = ^-3$.
(2) When y is 0, then $2x = 15$
    so $x = 7\frac{1}{2}$.

D5 Draw axes with x from $^-5$ to 15 and y from $^-5$ to 10.
   (a) Draw and label the graph of $x + 2y = 14$.
   (b) Draw and label the graph of $3x - 4y = 12$.
   (c) Write down the values of x and y where the graphs cross.
   (d) Check that these values fit both equations simultaneously.

D6 Solve each of these pairs of simultaneous equations graphically. (This means draw the graphs of the two equations and find the values of x and y which fit both equations.)

In some cases the values of x and y are not whole numbers. When that happens, estimate the values from the graph to 1 decimal place.

   (a) $2x - y = 10$
       $x + 3y = 12$
   (b) $4x - y = 10$
       $x + 2y = 8$

   (c) $2x - 3y = 15$
       $x - 4y = 10$
   (d) $2x + 5y = 20$
       $x - 3y = 3$

D7 Something peculiar happens when you try to solve these simultaneous equations graphically.

   $2x + 5y = 15$
   $4x + 10y = 20$

Describe what happens when you draw the two graphs. Can you see anything in the equations themselves which explains what happens?

D8 What happens when you try to solve these simultaneous equations graphically?

   $x + 5y = 10$
   $2x + 10y = 20$

Explain from the equations why it happens.

15 Investigations (2)

Counting the ways

You have red cubes and black cubes, each 1 cm by 1 cm by 1 cm.

1 There are 4 different towers you can make which are 2 cm tall.

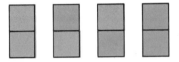

How many different ways are there to make a tower 3 cm tall?

Investigate for towers of different heights.

Is there any pattern in the numbers? Describe it.

Can you explain why you get the pattern?

2 This drawing shows a box with a lid.
Its inside is 3 cm by 2 cm by 1 cm.

Here is one way of arranging six
cubes in the box.

How many different arrangements
are there? Each cube can be red
or black.

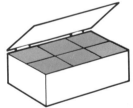

Investigate for other sizes of box.

*3 Here are nine cubes glued together
to make a '3 by 3' block.

There are 3 red cubes and
6 black cubes.

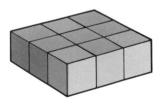

How many different 3 by 3 blocks can be made
from the 9 cubes shown here?

(**Note.** Two blocks which look the same when one is rotated, or
which look the same when one is turned over, are not to be
counted as different.)

16 Periodic graphs

A A mountain railway

A mountain railway runs from the base to the summit, a distance
of 4 km. There is only one railcar, and it takes 15 minutes for the
journey up and 10 minutes for the journey down.

When the car arrives at either station it waits for 5 minutes before
leaving again.

Throughout the day there is a regular pattern of service on the railway.
The graph below shows a part of it.

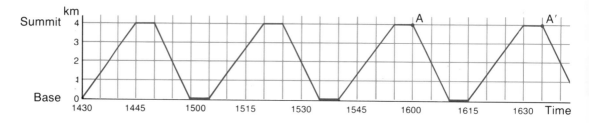

Anything which repeats itself at regular intervals is said to be **periodic**.
The service on the railway is periodic. The graph which shows the pattern
of the service is also said to be periodic.

If we take any point on the graph (say A) and look for the next point where
the pattern repeats exactly (A′), the time interval between A and A′ is
called the **period** of the graph.

A1 What is the period, in minutes, of the graph above?

A2 What is the period of each of these graphs?

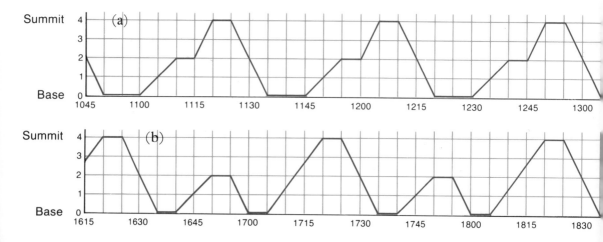

B Day and night

The table below shows how the number of hours of daylight varies
in London during the course of a year. The days of the year have been
numbered, so that day 1 is 1st January, and so on.

Day	1	21	41	61	81	101	121	141	161	181	201	221	241	261	281	301	321	341	361
Number of hours of daylight	7·9	8·5	9·7	11·0	12·3	13·6	14·9	15·9	16·6	16·7	16·0	15·0	13·8	12·5	11·2	9·9	8·7	7·9	7·8

B1 Draw a graph with axes numbered like this.

Plot the points from the table above and draw a smooth curve through them.

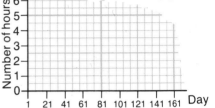

The pattern of the number of hours of daylight repeats itself every year.
Here is the graph for the years 1983–1987. The graph is periodic.

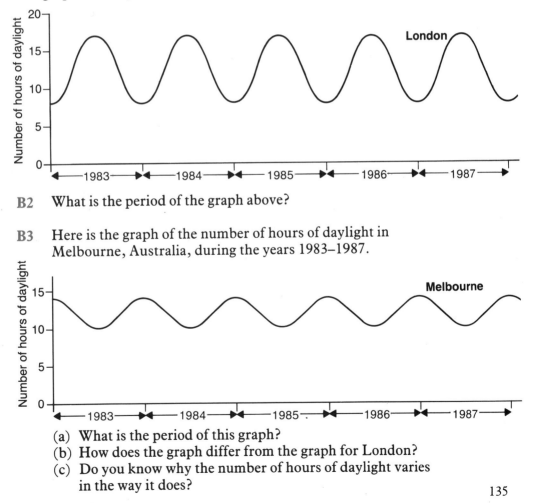

B2 What is the period of the graph above?

B3 Here is the graph of the number of hours of daylight in
Melbourne, Australia, during the years 1983–1987.

(a) What is the period of this graph?
(b) How does the graph differ from the graph for London?
(c) Do you know why the number of hours of daylight varies
in the way it does?

135

Why does the number of hours of daylight vary?

The Earth goes round the sun in 1 year (more accurately, 365·24 days).
The Earth's axis is tilted, and this has an effect on the number of
hours of daylight.

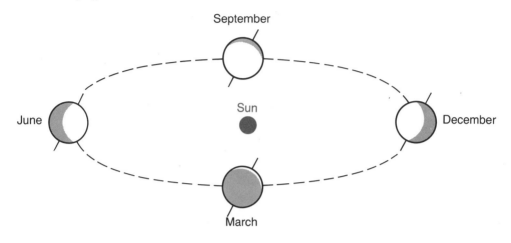

Here is the position of the Earth in June.
The north pole is tilted towards the sun.
(The tilting is exaggerated in this diagram, to make things clearer.)

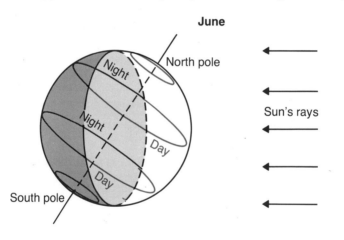

As the Earth rotates on its axis, places in the northern hemisphere spend
longer in sunlight than in shadow. In fact, close to the north pole
there is no darkness at all.

Places in the southern hemisphere spend longer in shadow than in
sunlight, and close to the south pole there is no sunlight at all:

So in June, places in the northern hemisphere have long days and
short nights. In the southern hemisphere it is the other way round.

In December, the position is reversed.

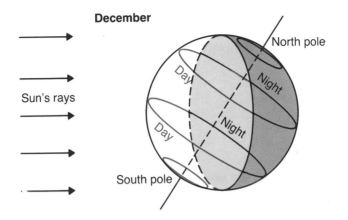

December

Sun's rays

North pole

Day

Night

Night

Day

South pole

In December, the northern hemisphere has short days and long nights, and the southern hemisphere has long days and short nights.

B4 These graphs show how the number of hours of daylight varies during the year in six places A, B, C, D, E and F.

Write the places in order, with the place furthest north first and the place furthest south last.

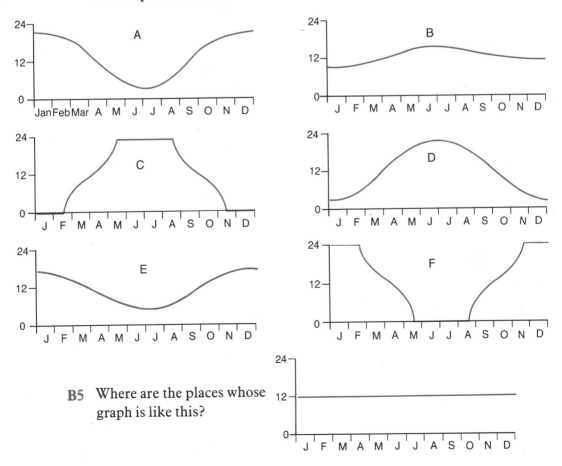

B5 Where are the places whose graph is like this?

B6 This table gives the times of sunrise and sunset in London during a year. The times are given in decimals of an hour instead of hours and minutes. (So, for example, 4·5 means 04:30.)
All the times are given as Greenwich Mean Time, instead of using British Summer Time for part of the year.

Day	1	21	41	61	81	101	121	141	161	181	201	221	241	261	281	301	321	341	361
Time of sunrise	8·1	7·9	7·4	6·7	6·0	5·2	4·5	4·0	3·7	3·7	4·1	4·6	5·1	5·6	6·2	6·8	7·4	7·9	8·1
Time of sunset	16·0	16·4	17·1	17·7	18·3	18·8	19·4	19·9	20·3	20·4	20·1	19·6	18·9	18·1	17·4	16·7	16·1	15·8	15·9

Draw the graphs of sunrise and sunset on the same pair of axes.
Number the axes as shown here.

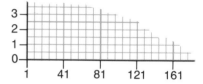

B7 Here are the sunrise and sunset graphs for three other places. Whereabouts on the Earth's surface is each place? Choose an answer from these five descriptions:

Close to north pole   In northern hemisphere   On the equator
In southern hemisphere   Close to south pole

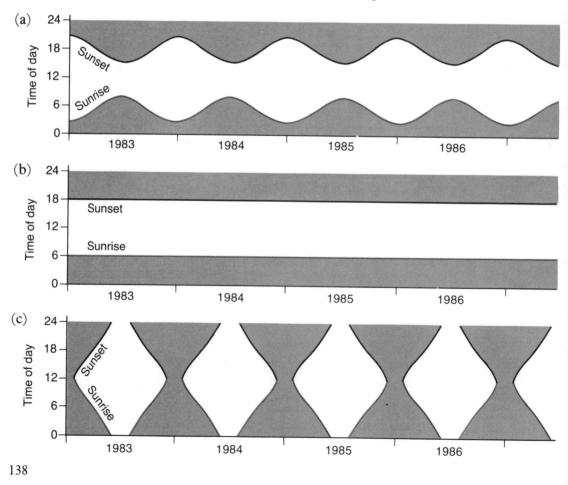

138

C Tides

Tides are caused by the gravitational pull of the sun and moon, so we
would expect graphs of tides to be periodic.
All around the world there are tidal gauges measuring the height of the tide.
Each gauge draws a graph. This graph shows 15 days of tidal changes at Dover.

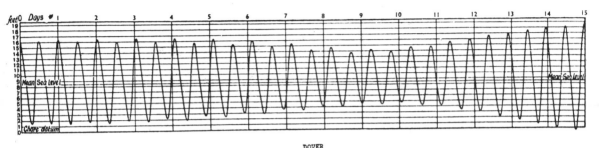

DOVER

C1 (a) The graph shows that high and low tides occur at regular intervals,
but the graph cannot be described as truly periodic. Why not?
(b) How many low tides occur in 15 days?
(c) Use your answer to (b) to calculate the number of hours between
each low tide and the next. Give your answer to 1 d.p.

On a day when the difference in height between high tide and low tide
is at its greatest, we say there is a **spring** tide. When the difference is at
its smallest value, we say there is a **neap** tide.

C2 (a) When did a neap tide occur during the 15 days at Dover?
(b) The graph shows that a spring tide occurred at some time
during the first 5 days, but it is not clear on which day it
happened. Decide for yourself which day it happened.

C3 This tidal graph for Avonmouth shows clearly how the height of the
tide varies. It looks 'spiky' because it covers many days in a short space.

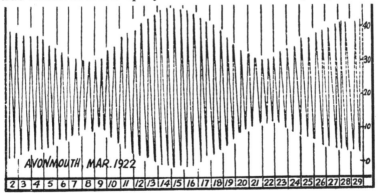

(a) On which day did a spring tide occur?
(b) Two neap tides are shown. When did they occur?
(c) How many feet did the water level rise at the spring tide?
(d) How many feet did it rise at the first neap tide?

139

Going into harbour

Ships must take great care going into harbour.
Some harbours dry out completely at low tide.

This harbour in the south of England is used by
large numbers of summer visitors. Some have
their own boats, some go on pleasure trips and
others use the ferry.

The graphs below show how the height of the water-level varies
on a day when there is a neap tide, and on a day when there is
a spring tide.

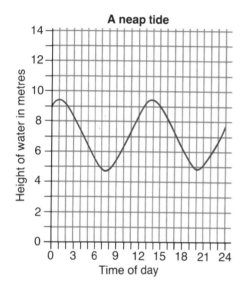

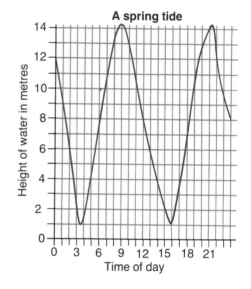

C4 How can you tell from the spring tide graph that the tide
takes longer to go out than to come in?

C5 Repairs have to be made to the harbour walls. The work can only
be done when the height of the water is less than 5 metres.

For how many hours out of 24 can the work be done when
there is   (a) a neap tide   (b) a spring tide

C6 The ferry boat has a depth of 1·5 m below the water line.
For how many hours can it use the harbour on a day when
there is   (a) a neap tide   (b) a spring tide

C7 A cargo boat is heading towards the harbour on the day of
the spring tide whose graph is shown above. The depth of
the boat below the water line is 4 m. She expects to arrive at 14:00.
How long will she have to wait to enter harbour?

Holy Island: how the tide affects access

Holy Island is situated off the coast of Northumberland. It is connected to the mainland by a road which is covered by the sea for part of the day.

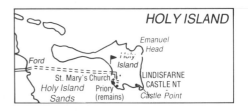

This graph shows how the height of the water above the level of the road changes.

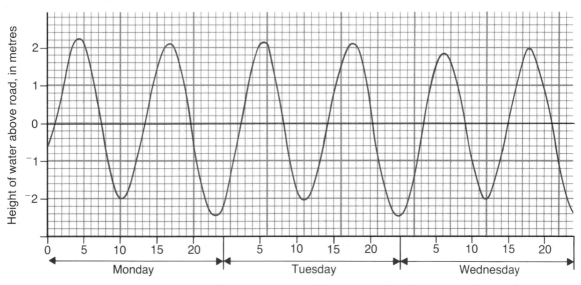

C8 (a) Estimate when the road first clears of water on Monday.
    (b) For how long is the road clear in the middle of Tuesday?
    (c) What is the deepest amount of water over the road at any time?

C9 A coach tour operator in Newcastle wants to run a day trip to Holy Island. The journey from the city takes 2 hours. Which of the three days shown on the graph do you think he should choose? Give your reasons.

C10 A family decide to go by car on Monday. The journey takes $1\frac{1}{2}$ hours. When would they have to leave home if they are to have as much time on the island as possible?

C11 If you arrive at the mainland end of the road to the island, what is the longest time you could have to wait before you cross?

C12 A hiker stays on the island and decides to leave on Tuesday afternoon. She is at the farthest tip of the island and needs 2 hours to get to the mainland. What is the latest time she can leave and still keep her feet dry?

If you have been to the seaside, you may have wondered
how a small boat, with no modern equipment, finds
its way into harbour at night. During the day, the
skipper can use a compass to take the bearings of objects
such as lighthouses, towers and churches. At night, he
can take the bearings of navigation lights. But first he
must know how to tell which light is which.

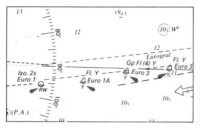

Navigation lights flash in different ways. By looking
at the type of flash and the time between flashes
it is possible to find out from special maps which
light you are looking at.

The map here shows some lights in the North Sea.
When you have worked through the question D1, you
may be able to work out what the symbols mean.

A graph can be used to show the pattern
of flashes of a navigation light.

This graph shows a light which flashes
twice every 10 seconds.

The period of the graph is 10 seconds.

D1 Here are descriptions of some standard types of navigation light.
On the opposite page are the graphs which match the descriptions.
Write down which description goes with each graph, and the period.

Fixed	A continuous steady light
Flashing	A light showing a single flash at regular intervals, the duration of light being always less than that of darkness
Fixed and flashing	A steady light with, at regular intervals, one flash of increased brilliance
Group flashing	At regular intervals two or more flashes in a group
Quick flashing	Flashing continuously more than 60 times a minute
Interrupted quick flashing	Flashing at a rate of more than 60 times a minute, with, at regular intervals, a total eclipse (darkness)
Occulting	A steady light with, at regular intervals, one sudden and total eclipse, the duration of darkness being always less than the duration of light
Group occulting	At regular intervals two or more sudden eclipses in a group
Isophase	A light where durations of light and darkness are equal

D2 Draw graphs for these lights.
(a) Flashing – period 4 s   (b) Group flashing – 3 flashes, period 20 s
(c) Occulting – eclipsed for 4 s, period 18 s

The time axes of these graphs are numbered in seconds.
The scales are not all the same.

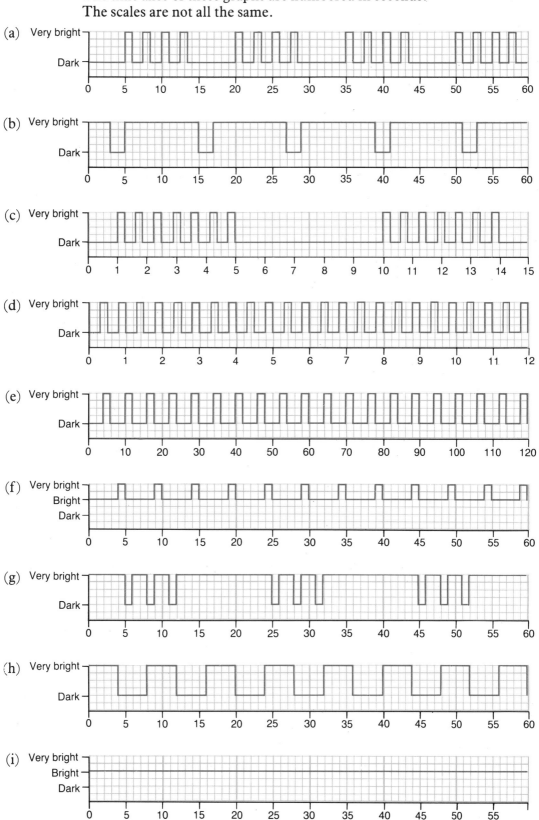

17 Probability

A Random selection

Rotating drums like this one are often used to
select the winner of a raffle. All the numbered
tickets are put into the drum, which is then
rotated to mix them all up. Then the drum is
opened and someone puts his hand in without
looking. He picks out a ticket and reads out
the winning number.

Suppose there are 200 tickets inside, numbered 1 to 200.
They are all mixed up, and the person who picks one is not looking.
Every ticket has an equal chance of being chosen.
We call this method of picking a ticket **random selection**.

Now suppose you have bought ticket number 68.
This ticket has 1 chance out of 200 of being the winner.

We write the chance of winning as a fraction, $\frac{1}{200}$, or a decimal, 0.005.

If you have bought two tickets, your chance of winning is 2 out of 200,

or $\frac{2}{200}$, which is equal to $\frac{1}{100}$ or 0.01.

> **A1** A drum contains 50 tickets numbered 1 to 50.
> One ticket is drawn by random selection from the drum.
> What is your chance of winning if you have bought
> tickets 36, 37 and 38? Write your answer as a fraction
> and as a decimal.

> **A2** What is your chance of winning (as a fraction and as
> a decimal) if you have bought
>
> (a) 1 ticket out of 40   (b) 7 tickets out of 40
> (c) 7 tickets out of 400   (d) 3 tickets out of 1000
> (e) 1 ticket out of 65   (f) 9 tickets out of 65
> (g) 1 ticket out of 100   (h) 5 tickets out of 500

> **A3** A bowl contains 100 ping-pong balls. Five of them are marked
> with a spot.
> A person selects a ball 'at random' by putting in his hand without
> looking, mixing up the balls, and picking one out.
>
> (a) What is the chance of picking out a ball with a spot?
> (b) What is the chance of picking out a ball without a spot?

Random selection does not have to be done by picking something out of a drum or bowl, etc. When you throw an ordinary dice, you are making a random selection of one number out of the six possible numbers 1 to 6.

Each of the six numbers has the same chance of coming up. So the chance of getting a four, say, is $\frac{1}{6}$.

A4 The faces of an ordinary dice are coloured as shown here. (The diagram shows the dice 'opened out' so that you can see every face.)

If the dice is thrown, what is the chance of getting   (a) a three   (b) a red face   (c) a black face

A5 If this spinner is spun, what is the chance of getting

(a) 6   (b) red   (c) black   (d) white

A6 In a game of bingo, the caller has a bowl, which to start with contains 90 balls, numbered 1 to 90. He selects a ball at random, calls out the number and puts the ball to one side. Then he makes another random selection from those that are left, and so on until the bowl is empty.

Each player has a card with 15 numbers on it and ticks off each number when it is called. The winner is the first to complete a card.

Jane is playing bingo. So far, ten numbers have been called, but none of them is on her card. What is the chance that the next number called is on her card?

Split the class up into pairs for this activity. Each pair needs a dice.

1 Call yourselves A and B.
A marks **either** two faces **or** four faces of the dice with a coloured spot. (Use a felt-tip pen so that it will come off later.) Do not tell B whether two or four faces have been marked.

2 A throws the dice where B cannot see it, and calls out 'yes' if a marked face comes up, and 'no' if not.

3 B keeps a tally of the number of 'yes' and 'no' calls. After 6 throws B guesses how many faces of the dice (two or four) are marked.
A does not tell B whether he or she is right or wrong.

4 After some more throws, B can change the guess, if he or she wants to. Throwing and guessing continue until B feels sure of the number of marked faces on the dice. Only then does A show B the dice.

B Probability

Think of a dice with 4 red faces and 2 black faces.
When the dice is thrown, red is more likely to come up than black.
In fact, red is twice as likely to come up.

The chance, or **probability**, of getting red is $\frac{4}{6}$ or $\frac{2}{3}$, and the
probability of getting black is $\frac{2}{6}$ or $\frac{1}{3}$.

In a very long run of throws, we would expect the number of red to be
about twice the number of black. In other words, we would expect
about $\frac{2}{3}$ of the throws to be red and about $\frac{1}{3}$ black.

Earlier on (in Book Y1) you found the probability that a
drawing pin lands point upwards, by **experiment**.
You threw the pin many times and counted the results.

With a dice you can find probabilities by just **looking at it**.
It is a cube with 6 identical faces, so the probability of each face
coming up is the same, $\frac{1}{6}$.

You cannot just look at a drawing pin and say what the probability is
that it will fall point upwards.

> **B1** A regular tetrahedron has 4 identical faces. Three of them
> are red. If the tetrahedron is thrown, what is the probability
> that it will land on a red face?

> **B2** A regular octahedron has 3 red faces and 5 black faces.
> If it is rolled, what is the probability that it lands with
> a red face on top?

There are six ways in which an ordinary dice can fall.
They are called the six **equally likely outcomes** for one throw of the dice.
They are, of course, 1, 2, 3, 4, 5, 6.

Suppose you want to know the probability that the number thrown is
greater than 4.
This is the same as the probability that the number is 5 or 6.

'The number thrown is greater than 4' is called an **event**. It is something
which may or may not happen. The outcomes 5 and 6 are said to be
favourable to this event.

The probability of an event is the fraction $\dfrac{\text{Number of favourable outcomes}}{\text{Total number of equally likely outcomes}}$.

When you are calculating the probability of an event, first make a list of
all the equally likely outcomes. Then list or tick off the favourable outcomes.
Then work out the probability. This may seem long-winded at first, but
it will help you to avoid mistakes later.

Worked example

A bag contains four 1p coins, five 2p coins, three 5p coins and three 10p coins.
A coin is drawn at random. What is the probability that its value is
more than 4p?

Equally likely outcomes: 1   1   1   1   2   2   2   2   2   5   5   5   10   10   10
Favourable outcomes: √   √   √   √   √   √

There are 6 favourable outcomes out of 15 equally likely outcomes.
So the probability is $\frac{6}{15} = \frac{2}{5}$.
(Notice that each individual coin is an equally likely outcome.)

B3 In my hand I hold eight cards, numbered 2, 3, 4, 5, 6, 7, 8, 9.
My friend picks a card at random. What is the probability
(a) that he picks a number less than 4
(b) that he picks a number divisible by 3
(c) that he picks a prime number

B4 In Polly's handbag there are six £5 notes, four £10 notes, five £20 notes
and a £50 note, all mixed up. She takes out a note at random.
(a) What is the probability that she takes out more than £10?
(b) What is the probability that she takes out less than £10?

B5 A drum contains 100 raffle tickets numbered 1 to 100. One ticket is
drawn at random. What is the probability that the number drawn is
(a) a one-figure number   (b) a two-figure number
(c) a three-figure number   (d) a four-figure number

B6 In a raffle with 100 tickets, Jack has bought ticket number 58
and Jill has bought ticket number 7.

Who is right? Explain.

This is a class activity. Each person needs two coins.

Ray: If you throw two coins together, what is the probability that
          you get a head and a tail?
Sue: Well. There are 3 outcomes: 2 heads, head-and-tail, 2 tails.
          Only one outcome is favourable. So the probability is $\frac{1}{3}$.

Do you agree with Sue? Let each person in the class throw 2 coins many times.
Record the total number of throws and the number of times you get head-and-tail.

C Throwing coins

When you throw two coins you can get 2 heads, head-and-tail, or 2 tails. But these are **not** equally likely outcomes. You get head-and-tail more often than either 2 heads or 2 tails.

There is a reason for this. Call the two coins A and B, and think of all the different ways the two coins can fall. There are 4 ways:

A head, B head   A head, B tail   A tail, B head   A tail, B tail

These are the **4** equally likely outcomes when you throw the two coins. **2** of the outcomes are favourable to the event 'throwing 1 head and 1 tail'. So the probability of throwing 1 head and 1 tail is $\frac{2}{4}$ or $\frac{1}{2}$.

C1 If two coins are thrown
- (a) what is the probability of getting 2 heads?
- (b) what is the probability of getting 2 tails?

C2 Three coins are thrown. Call them A, B and C.

A	B	C
H	H	H
H	H	T

and so on

- (a) Make a list of all the different equally likely outcomes. It is quicker to make a table, as shown on the right.

- (b) How many of the equally likely outcomes are favourable to the event '1 head and 2 tails are thrown'?
- (c) What is the probability of getting 1 head and 2 tails, in any order?
- (d) What is the probability of getting 2 heads and 1 tail, in any order?
- (e) What is the probability of getting   (i) 3 heads   (ii) 3 tails?

C3 Four coins are thrown.
- (a) Make a list of all the equally likely outcomes. (You will find it helpful to start from the list for three coins.)
- (b) What is the probability of getting   (i) 0 heads and 4 tails   (ii) 1 head and 3 tails   (iii) 2 heads and 2 tails   (iv) 3 heads and 1 tail   (v) 4 heads and 0 tails

C4 This table shows the number of equally likely outcomes when 1, 2, 3, 4 coins are thrown.

Number of coins thrown	1	2	3	4
Number of equally likely outcomes	2	4	8	16

- (a) How many equally likely outcomes are there when 5 coins are thrown?
- (b) How many of them are favourable to the event '5 heads are thrown'?
- (c) What is the probability of getting 5 heads when 5 coins are thrown?
- (d) A football team has 7 matches to play. What is the probability that they will win the toss in all 7 of them?

D Throwing two dice

Split the class up into pairs. Each pair needs two dice.

When you throw two dice, the total score can be 2, 3, 4, 5, 6, 7, 8, 9, 10, 11 or 12. Throw two dice several times and count the number of times you get each of the possible total scores. Collect together the results for the whole class.

Which of these frequency graphs do your results look like most?

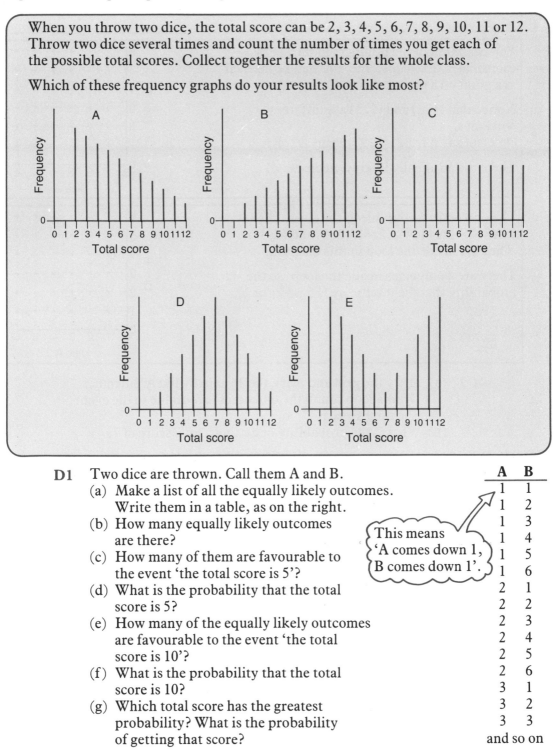

D1 Two dice are thrown. Call them A and B.

(a) Make a list of all the equally likely outcomes. Write them in a table, as on the right.

(b) How many equally likely outcomes are there?

(c) How many of them are favourable to the event 'the total score is 5'?

(d) What is the probability that the total score is 5?

(e) How many of the equally likely outcomes are favourable to the event 'the total score is 10'?

(f) What is the probability that the total score is 10?

(g) Which total score has the greatest probability? What is the probability of getting that score?

This means 'A comes down 1, B comes down 1'.

A	B
1	1
1	2
1	3
1	4
1	5
1	6
2	1
2	2
2	3
2	4
2	5
2	6
3	1
3	2
3	3
and so on	

149

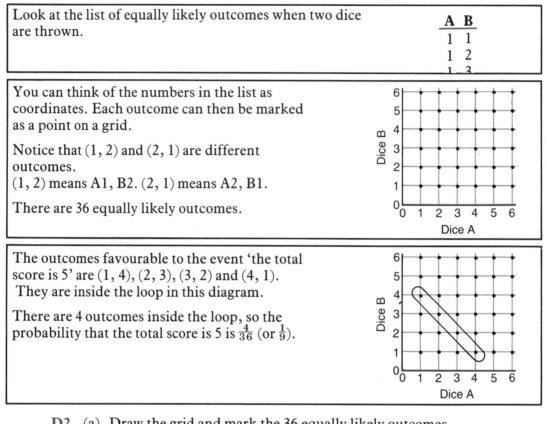

Look at the list of equally likely outcomes when two dice are thrown.

A	B
1	1
1	2
1	3

You can think of the numbers in the list as coordinates. Each outcome can then be marked as a point on a grid.

Notice that (1, 2) and (2, 1) are different outcomes.
(1, 2) means A1, B2. (2, 1) means A2, B1.

There are 36 equally likely outcomes.

The outcomes favourable to the event 'the total score is 5' are (1, 4), (2, 3), (3, 2) and (4, 1). They are inside the loop in this diagram.

There are 4 outcomes inside the loop, so the probability that the total score is 5 is $\frac{4}{36}$ (or $\frac{1}{9}$).

D2 (a) Draw the grid and mark the 36 equally likely outcomes. Draw a loop round the outcomes favourable to the event 'the total score is 7'.
(b) What is the probability of getting a total score of 7?

D3 (a) (4, 5) is one of the outcomes favourable to the event 'the total score is 9'. What are the others?
(b) What is the probability of getting a total score of 9?

D4 Copy and complete this table of probabilities.

Total score with two dice	2	3	4	5	6	7	8	9	10	11	12
Probability				$\frac{4}{36}$							

D5 (a) How many outcomes are favourable to the event 'the total score is greater than 9'?
(b) What is the probability that the total score is greater than 9?
(c) How can you get this probability from the table in question D4?

D6 (a) Draw the grid again and mark the 36 outcomes. Draw a loop round all the outcomes favourable to the event 'the scores on the two dice are equal'.
(b) What is the probability that the scores on the dice are equal?

D7 Instead of looking at the sum of the two scores, we can look at the difference between them.

For the outcome (3, 5), the difference is 2.

For the outcome (5, 3), the difference is also 2.

(Take the smaller score from the larger each time.)

For the outcome (4, 4), the difference is 0.

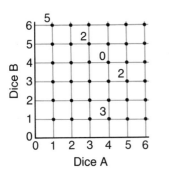

Dice B (vertical axis), Dice A (horizontal axis)

(a) Draw a grid and mark the 36 outcomes. Against each outcome write the difference for that outcome.

Some of them are shown here.

(b) How many outcomes are favourable to the event 'the difference between the scores is 2'?

(c) What is the probability that the difference is 2?

(d) Find the probability of each other difference and write the results in a table.

Difference between scores on two dice	0	1	2	3	4	5
Probability						

E Miscellaneous questions

E1 Peach's Encyclopedia is in three volumes, I, II, and III. Sam takes the three volumes out of a bag at random. He puts them on a shelf in the order in which they come out of the bag.

(a) Make a list of all the different equally likely arrangements of the three volumes on the shelf (for example, I, II, III; II, I, III; etc.).

(b) What is the probability that the three volumes are in the correct order (from left to right)?

(c) What is the probability that volume I is in the correct position?

E2 The four volumes of General Fiasco's memoirs are taken at random and put on a shelf. What is the probability that

(a) volume 4 is in the correct position

(b) volume 3 is in the correct position

(c) volume 1 comes before volume 2 (from left to right)

(d) every volume is in its correct position (from left to right)

(e) volumes 2 and 3 are in their correct positions

E3 Volumes 1 and 2 of General Fiasco's memoirs have red covers and volumes 3 and 4 have blue covers.

If the four volumes are taken at random and put on a shelf, what is the probability that

(a) the two red books are side by side

(b) the two blue books are side by side

(c) the red books are side by side and so are the blue books

Review 3

12 Proportionality

12.1 A cookery book gives these instructions for roasting pork:
25 minutes per pound, plus an extra 35 minutes.

(a) Which of these sketch graphs shows the relationship between
the weight of a joint and its cooking time?

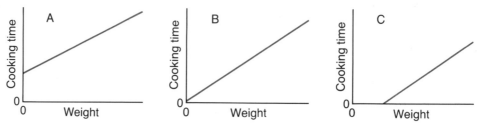

(b) Is the cooking time proportional to the weight?

12.2 A variable q is proportional to another variable p.
Copy and complete this table of values of p and q.
Give each value correct to 1 decimal place.

p	3·8	5·3	
q	10·1		25·6

12.3 In a process for copper-plating saucepans, the mass of copper
deposited is proportional to the time for which the process is
allowed to continue.
After 15 minutes, the mass deposited is 7·8 grams.
How much longer will it take for the mass to reach 20 grams?

12.4 This graph shows the relationship
between two variables u and v.

Find the equation connecting u and v.

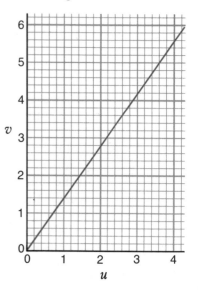

12.5 A student measured the volumes of six pieces of lead and weighed each piece. Here are her results.

Volume in cm³	0·8	1·4	1·8	2·2	2·6	3·0
Mass in grams	9·1	15·9	20·4	26·9	29·5	34·0

(a) Draw axes on graph paper and plot the six points.

(b) The student made an error in measuring either the volume or the mass of one of the pieces of lead. Put a ring round the incorrect point.

(c) Draw the straight line through (0, 0) which best fits the five remaining points.

(d) Calculate the gradient of the line of best fit.

(e) What does the value of the gradient tell you about the lead?

13 Area

13.1 Calculate the area of each of these shapes.

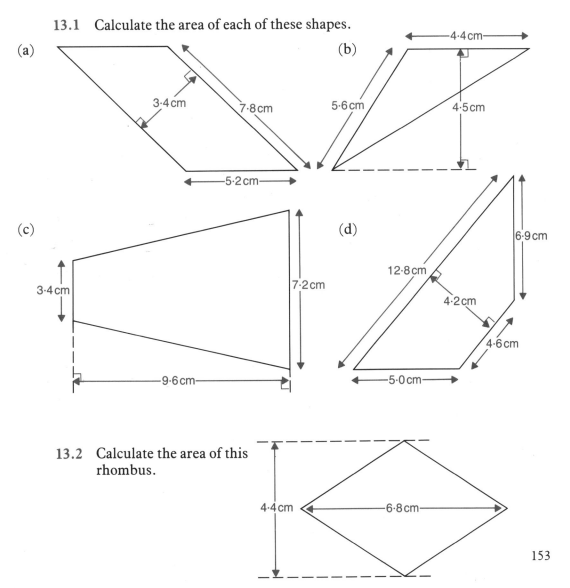

13.2 Calculate the area of this rhombus.

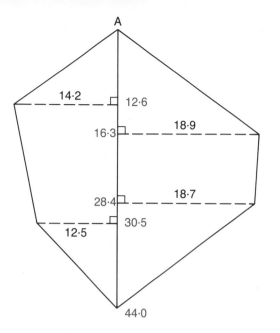

13.3 This sketch plan shows the measurements made in an offset survey of a piece of land.

All distances are in metres. Those in red are distances measured from the point A.

Calculate the area of the piece of land correct to the nearest square metre.

13.4 (a) Calculate the area of a circle of radius $5 \cdot 8\,$cm, to the nearest $0 \cdot 1\,$cm^2.
   (b) Calculate the area of a circle of diameter $5 \cdot 8\,$cm, to the nearest $0 \cdot 1\,$cm^2.
   (c) Calculate the radius of a circle of area $20\,$cm^2, to the nearest $0 \cdot 1\,$cm.

13.5 A farmer has 50 metres of wire fencing. If he uses it to enclose a circle, calculate   (a) the radius   (b) the area of the circle.

13.6 A farmer wants to enclose an area of $100\,$m^2. She has a choice between a square enclosure and a circular enclosure.
   (a) What length of fencing would she need for a square enclosure?
   (b) What length would she need for a circular enclosure?
   (c) If she buys just enough fencing for a circular enclosure of area $100\,$m^2, but then decides to use it to make a square enclosure, what area will she be able to enclose?

14 Linear equations and inequalities

14.1 Draw axes with x and y from 0 to 10.

   (a) Draw and label the graphs of $2x + 5y = 10$, $2x + 5y = 15$ and $2x + 5y = 20$.

   (b) Label clearly the region where $2x + 5y < 10$ and the region where $2x + 5y > 20$.

14.2 A market garden sells apples in large boxes, holding 6 kg, and small boxes, holding 3 kg. They will not accept orders for less than 15 kg, and they deliver free any orders of more than 30 kg.

Suppose an order consists of x large boxes and y small boxes.
(a) Write down an expression for the total weight of the order in terms of x and y.
(b) Write down the equation which says that the total weight of the order is 15 kg.
(c) Write the equation which says that the total weight is 30 kg.
(d) Draw axes with x and y from 0 to 12.
Draw the two lines whose equations you have written down. Label the region of the graph which contains all the points for which the order will not be accepted, and the region where delivery will be free.

14.3 Draw axes with x and y from 0 to 12.
Draw the graphs of $3x + 4y = 18$ and $x + 3y = 12$.
Write down the values of x and y which fit both equations simultaneously, as accurately as you can from the graph.

14.4 Solve these pairs of simultaneous equations graphically.
(a) $2x - 5y = 15$ (b) $2x - 5y = 15$
    $3x + y = 3$ $^{-}3x + y = 3$

16 Periodic graphs

16.1 The moon rises and sets each day. (Sometimes we do not see it rise or set because it happens in daylight.) The table below gives the number of hours for which the moon is out (the length of moonshine) every two days for 71 days.

Day	Time in hours	Day	Time in hours	Day	Time in hours	Day	Time in hours
1	12·5	19	16·1	37	7·8	55	13·5
3	10·5	21	17·3	39	9·2	57	11·4
5	8·7	23	17·0	41	10·9	59	9·5
7	7·6	25	16·2	43	12·8	61	8·1
9	7·6	27	14·3	45	14·8	63	7·6
11	8·6	29	12·0	47	16·6	65	8·2
13	10·3	31	10·0	49	17·3	67	9·6
15	12·2	33	8·4	51	16·4	69	11·4
17	14·2	35	7·5	53	15·5	71	13·4

Draw a graph to show how the length of moonshine varies, and estimate the period of the graph in days.

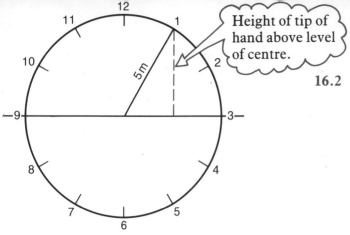

Height of tip of hand above level of centre.

16.2 The minute hand of a large clock is 5 metres long.

Draw a diagram to a scale of 1 cm to 1 metre. Measure the height of the tip of the hand above the level of the centre of the clock at each hour from noon to midnight.

Draw a graph of (time, height of tip above centre).

Draw a sketch to show how the graph continues.

17 Probability

17.1 Janet has these cards in her hand:

Ace of spades, Ace of hearts, Queen of clubs, Jack of hearts, 10 of hearts, 7 of clubs, 6 of clubs, 6 of diamonds, 3 of spades, 3 of hearts, 3 of diamonds, 2 of diamonds.

Sandra takes one card at random. What is the probability that it is
(a) an ace   (b) a spade   (c) the Queen of clubs   (d) a 3   (e) a diamond

17.2 Two five-sided spinners are each numbered 1 to 5.
(a) Draw a grid and mark points on it to show all the equally likely outcomes when both spinners are spun.
(b) Draw a loop round all the outcomes for which the total score is more than 5.
(c) What is the probability that the total score is more than 5?

M Miscellaneous

M1 A couple wish to cover the floor of a rectangular room 5·8 m by 3·4 m with plain carpet.
They think that the cheapest way to do it is to buy a 'remnant', which is a rectangular piece of carpet they can cut up.
The shop has three remnants in stock.
        A is 5·5 m by 4·2 m and costs £110.
        B is 4·9 m by 3·7 m and costs £90.
        C is 8·2 m by 2·5 m and costs £90.
(a) Which remnant is made from the most expensive material?
(b) Which is made from the cheapest material?
(c) Which remnants could be used to carpet their room?
(d) Show how each of these could be cut. It is best to have as few cuts as possible in the carpet on the floor.